SUCCESS IN THE YEAR OF THE OX

[2021]

D1304364

Linda Dearsley

DARK
RIVER

TABLE OF CONTENTS

CHAPTER 1: SUCCESS IN THE YEAR OF THE OX

Welcome to the Year of the Ox, which muscles its way in on the 12th of February 2021, and barrels on through until the 31st of January 2022.

If you're still feeling shell-shocked after the roller-coaster ride that was 2020 – brought to us courtesy of the ever-restless Rat – you're not alone. And, after the incredible events of the past year, you're probably wondering what on earth 2021 will bring. Well, there's good news and some not quite so good news on the horizon.

The good news is that thanks to the Ox, life in 2021 promises to be a little calmer and quieter than last year. The less good news, depending on the strength of your nerves, is that this particular Year of the Ox is known as the White or Golden Ox – because this Ox arrives as a close companion to his furry friend of 2020 (the Golden Rat) since they both share the same element – Metal.

Because of this, despite the enormous differences in their sizes and temperaments, this gilded pair have a lot in common; so, don't expect the changes and controversies of last year to disappear on the stroke of midnight.

On the other hand, now that we're – hopefully – all getting used to the upheaval that's come our way, we can allow ourselves a long sigh of relief as the exhausting Rat finally scuttles off into the sunset and we can settle down to appreciate the steadier, more reassuring Year of the Ox.

The Revolution's Begun

To get a handle on what's in store in 2021, it's important to understand what just happened over the last 12 months. 2020 – the Year of the Golden Rat – wasn't just any old average year. It was always destined to be a major event – a massive turning point for the entire world.

For once, the systems of both East and West were in agreement about its huge significance. This is unusual because, in the West, we measure our years in decades and tend to think of each decade as different from the one before, of having its own distinct character. The 1920's were reckoned to be quite different from the 1930's, which in turn were quite different from the 1940's, and so on. And for that reason, the year that opens the new decade – the first of the ten – is regarded as a bit special, the harbinger of the changes to come.

It's the same in the East except, in Chinese astrology, these bundles of years are measured in cycles of twelve, not tens, and that special first year of the new cycle is always the Year of the Rat. It's the job of the frenetic Rat to kick-start the changes that set the tone for the new era to come.

But what made 2020, the Year of the Golden Rat, so momentous was that the new era in the East coincided with a new decade in the West – turbo-charging the energy for change around the planet. So rare is it for the two systems to be in sync – due to the difference in counting in tens as opposed to counting in twelves – it's 60 years, well over half a century, since such an event occurred before. The last time the two systems overlapped in this way was in 1960 – the start of the decade that changed the world.

So, the Year of the Golden Rat was always destined to have a big impact. And the chances are, whatever happened in 2020 wasn't a blip, a minor hiccough before things get back to normal – it was year one of our brave new world.

The Power of Metal

Rat years always bring a change of course, and thanks to the combining of the new eras in the East and in the West, it was only to be expected that the changes of 2020 would be *much more* powerful and far-reaching than in an average Rat year.

The fact that it was a metal Rat year provided a clue as to the form the changes might take. Metal is overwhelmingly associated with money and finance in Chinese astrology, so big upheavals – both good and bad – in economics and employment are to be expected.

Intriguingly, the element metal is also associated with the lungs in the Chinese tradition, so changes set in motion throughout the world by the arrival of the dreadful Covid-19 pandemic, which affected the lungs in severe cases, are not surprising in hindsight.

It looks as if the Rat used the tool of a virus, which affected the lungs, as the catalyst for the revolutionary changes to come.

And Now Here comes the Ox

It's quite normal to wake to a slight atmosphere of chaos when dawn breaks on a new Ox year. This is only to be expected after all the changes the outgoing Rat has set in motion. Rather like the disarray in a house the morning after a boisterous party, or maybe the state of a street after an unruly demonstration has passed through, a certain amount of debris is bound to be left behind. You can't make an omelet without breaking eggs, as they say.

This is where the healing energy of the strong and patient Ox comes into its own. The Ox is always number two in the cycle. Ox is quite accustomed to following on from the riotous Rat, and Ox's job is not to reverse the work of its rodent comrade; it's more to clear up, smooth over the changes, bed them in, and ensure they're operating efficiently.

This year, of course, we're left with chaos times ten, so we need the ministrations of the calming Ox more than ever. While 2021 promises to continue with many of the changes that were begun last year, they should play out in a gentler, more measured way.

Your Chance to Reboot Your Future

So what will the Year of the Golden Ox bring for you? After the confusions and possibly unexpected silver linings of last year, can you expect Golden good fortune to light your path as you dance through 2021? Or will you find yourself plodding flat-footed through the months, struggling to make your mark in the new landscape? Well, it all depends. According to Chinese astrology, it's up to you and the way you play your cards. Whatever the year, you'll get the chance to shape your own destiny – as long as you go about it in the right way.

The Year Influences the Events

Despite everything, there are plenty of fantastic opportunities on offer in the year of the Ox. Just as, despite the dramas, some people did very well in 2020 and created new ways of working and interacting, which became surprisingly empowering. So, in this year, these new approaches can be built-on and expanded. People who missed out in 2020 can learn from the success stories of last year and change tack in the months to come. To make the most of the good fortune, though, you need to get your head around the Chinese way of looking at these things – which is quite different from what we're used to in the West.

Whereas in the West, we tend to think of each new year as anonymous and impartial – an unwritten book just waiting for events to fill in the blank pages and establish a theme – in Chinese astrology it's just the opposite.

No year in Chinese astrology *is ever anonymous*. Each arrives bristling with its own unique animal 'personality' – fully formed and ready to rock, from day one.

In the East, the events don't influence the year – the year influences the events.

So, every Chinese New Year's Day, a totally different animal energy is unleashed on the world – and if you understand the effect that energy might have, you're more likely to work out what to expect and how to benefit.

Circumstances that might have led to dangerous disputes in a fiery Tiger year could pass by with scarcely a ripple when peaceful Rabbit's running the show. A laid-back, eat, drink and be merry approach might work wonders when carefree Pig's at the helm, but try it on in a conscientious Dog year, and such laziness could spell disaster. It really pays to know what you're dealing with!

Order is Restored

Last year, even when we were locked down waiting for the virus to pass, many people could still sense the frenetic energy in the air. Though they were becalmed at home, they couldn't seem to relax (they said). This is typical of the influence of the Rat – busily working away behind the scenes, endlessly creating changes. Even if those changes can't be seen, they can be felt.

But even the industrious Rat can't keep up this pace forever. At the end of a Rat year, we can feel wrung out and in need of a change of gear, which is where the substantial figure of the Ox stomps in. The Ox exudes a quieter energy – a chance to slow down and catch your breath. Ox does not intend to be rushed. There may still be change, but an invisible foot has been lifted off the accelerator when Ox is at the wheel.

Suddenly, cutting corners and shoddy workmanship won't be tolerated. Attempts to wriggle out of obligations will have consequences, and a fresh appreciation for traditional values of the past will dawn.

The Opulent Golden Ox

Yet, just like people, not all Oxen are the same. The Chinese zodiac acknowledges that while all Ox years will share the same basic Ox characteristics, there will be a subtle difference in emphasis to reflect the personality of the particular Ox in charge that year.

Zodiac Ox – like all the creatures of the Chinese calendar – come in five different varieties, or breeds, you might say – each with their own unique ways of expressing their distinctive characters. There are Water Ox, Wood Ox, Fire Ox, Earth Ox, and Metal Ox. 2021 is the Year of the Metal Ox – sharing the same element as last year's Rat – which is why 2021 is also known as the Year of the White or Golden Ox... the colors (white or gold) representing the Metal element in Chinese astrology. But, for our purposes, let's think of the Ox of 2021, like the Rat of 2020, as being Gold.

It's been over half a century since the last Golden Ox strolled impressively over the horizon – a magnificent, opulent creature imprinting the year with indelible Ox characteristics. So what kind of events did the last Golden Ox – of 1961 – inspire that might give us a clue as to what to expect in the coming 12 months?

Introducing the Groovy Golden Ox of 1961

As 1961 got underway, the USA was already experiencing the changes wrought by 1960's Rat. The brand new, youthful president, President John F. Kennedy, had just been inaugurated, and after the excitement of the previous year's election, the public was settling down to see if he'd live up to his early promise. In Britain, it didn't seem as if much had changed. Harold Macmillan was still Prime Minister, but beneath the surface, the seeds of drama were being sown.

1961 was the year British government minister John Profumo met a certain goodtime girl – Christine Keeler – at a party at Lord Astor's country seat, by the Thames (the impressive stately home known as Cliveden). Profumo, by all accounts, was entranced by the beautiful young woman. But, he was married, and this was the year of the family-oriented, traditional values Ox. Bearing that in mind, a liaison was unlikely to end well. It didn't.

Unknown to Profumo, the beguiling Ms. Keeler was also involved with a Russian Naval attaché – who could perhaps have been a spy. The resulting affair, kept secret for months, was to lead to a huge political scandal and court case a couple of years later. Indeed, the fall out damaged the government and shocked the nation.

Intriguingly, just a few days before Profumo's fateful meeting that summer, and little more than 100 miles away from Cliveden, a baby girl named Diana Spencer – Lady Diana Spencer – came into the world, in Norfolk, on July 1st. A month later, on August 4th, a healthy infant boy was born in sunny Honolulu. His parents called him Barack.

Had these tiny children been born a decade or so earlier, history may never have heard of them again. Yet the '60's changed attitudes so fast that young Diana was able to grow up to become the first 'commoner' (as she was described at the time) to marry a Prince of Wales. Little Barack, meanwhile, was destined to become the first black President of the USA.

As well as family, other Ox-like enthusiasms involve building, so it's not surprising that, in Germany, the Berlin Wall was being constructed fast.

When Berlin was divided into Communist-run East Germany and capitalist West Germany, the new East Germans began voting with their feet. They'd experienced change right enough, and they didn't like it. Around 1,000 citizens a day – every day – headed for the West, many of them professionals and skilled workers, an exodus that could have had disastrous consequences for the fledgling economy. The only way to keep these unhappy people in the country, it seemed, was to build a big wall patrolled by armed guards. That wall was to divide the nation for nearly 30 years.

Yet, the desire for change instigated in the previous Rat year remained strong, and in some places, desperate bids for freedom succeeded. There were numerous daring escapes from East Berlin, the first (just two days after the wall was erected) saw a 19-year-old border guard – Corporal Conrad Schumann – leap over a 3-foot high barrier of barbed wire before fleeing to the west.

Meanwhile, in Paris, famous Russian ballet star Rudolph Nureyev – on tour with the Kirov Ballet – was also chafing at the restrictions. One day, he gave his minders the slip and requested asylum in France. It was granted, much to the chagrin of his home country.

But, of course, the Soviet Union also enjoyed its triumphs. The whole world marveled when the news broke that Russia had launched the first human-crewed spacecraft into the starry sky. Blurry pictures were beamed back to earth of brave cosmonaut Yuri Gagarin orbiting the planet in Vostok 1, and Yuri became an international celebrity.

No doubt, this success spurred President Kennedy to step up the USA's own space program and the space race – which was to end with the first man on the Moon before the decade was out – hotted up.

There were no serious epidemics that year – a deadly pandemic of Asian flu had already struck back in 1957/58 – so, in 1961, the metal element seems to have been expressed in the vast amounts of money splashed around on space exploration and military hardware.

Russia exploded a huge nuclear bomb – nicknamed the Tsar Bomba – on Novaya Zemlya (an island in the Arctic). The resulting blast registered five on the Richter scale. The event was worrying enough to cause President Kennedy to go on TV to suggest that his fellow American families should build fall-out shelters in their backyards to protect them from nuclear radiation. DIY bomb shelter kits began to be offered for sale in home magazines – some made of plywood. Quite a few families took his advice.

The CIA, meanwhile, was secretly trying to reverse the changes in Cuba where the revolutionary – Fidel Castro – had taken power, nationalized American owned businesses, and aligned himself with the Soviet Union. The CIA financed and trained a unit of Cuban exiles to invade their old homeland in an attempt to depose Castro. In April 1961, the exiles landed in the South West of the island in the Bay of Pigs.

Unluckily for them, Castro's forces beat them back. One hundred and eighteen exile soldiers were killed, 1,200 captured, and the victorious Castro was regarded in Cuba as a national hero. This was another change that would stand for many years.

Away from the confusing world of politics, sensible, practical Ox qualities were coming to the fore. The conscientious dads who spent endless weekends building bomb shelters to protect their families would have earned the full support of the loyal Ox. The fact that the shelters were never to be used made no difference. It was the thought and the effort that counted.

Inspired by the same energy, inventors brought us the first electric toothbrush, the first disposable nappies, and the first hatchback car – the Renault 4 – that year, as well as the introduction of the contraceptive pill. All sensible, practical innovations, and perfectly in tune with the modern era that was taking shape.

Yet, the flashy metal element was still bubbling beneath the surface. Practical did not have to be plain or unsightly. Useful could be beautiful, too. One of the most sought-after and desired luxury cars – the E-Type Jaguar – made its debut in 1961, while the same year, legendary movie star Audrey Hepburn was inviting cinema goers to *Breakfast at Tiffany's* (a movie centering around the famous upmarket 5th Avenue jewelry store). The film was a big hit though, oddly, the Oscar it earned was not for the acting but for the music. *Moon River* by Henry Mancini and Johnny Mercer won best original song. The evocative composition remains popular to this day.

At home, families sat down to watch wholesome, traditional TV shows such as the westerns *Wagon Train*, *Gunsmoke*, and defender of justice, the honest, hotshot lawyer *Perry Mason*. But the changes of the '60s were still quietly unfurling. 1961 was the year the cult TV series *The Avengers* emerged. It was an original and quirky show that was to go on to define the fashions and mood of the new age, and grow and grow in popularity over the next few years.

Intriguingly, 1961 was also the year the first-ever report of an alien abduction gained publicity all over the world. Respectable civil servants Betty and Barney Hill, of New Hampshire, USA, were returning home from a holiday at Niagara Falls one September night, when they spotted a strange light in the sky.

They were driving along a lonely stretch of road in the White Mountains, and there were no other vehicles or buildings in sight. It almost looked as if this peculiar aircraft was following them. Later, they were to recall – under hypnosis – that the light turned out to be a flying saucer, which landed in front of their car. They described small alien beings with large eyes taking them aboard the craft, and subjecting them to medical examinations, before allowing them to return to their car and complete their journey.

Their account caused a sensation. Sceptics dismissed their story as a dream or hallucination, but the Hill's experiences were told and retold around the globe. There were books and a film about the affair. The public fascination with UFOs and aliens that was born that year shows no signs of abating.

Keep Calm and Carry On

If ever there was a motto that summed up the philosophy of the Ox, the famous Churchillian, 'Keep Calm and Carry On', couldn't be improved upon. Looking back now, we can see that – in 1961 – the previous year's upheavals were seldom reversed, but most of the time, a way was found to adopt them into everyday life until they became the new 'normal'. A few stubbornly determined individuals, who just couldn't tolerate the changed circumstances, were able to break away and begin again, but such rebellion could be dangerous and involved a huge effort. The kind of effort was something that not many would be prepared to undertake.

So, this is likely to be the shape of 2021. Chances are, we haven't quite seen the last of Covid-19, as the lung-affecting metal element is still swirling around. But the strength, ferocity, and speed of the challenge should diminish under the quieter influence of the Ox. Plus, we have begun to learn how to cope. The Ox will ensure that those who put the lessons into practice, and do the right thing, are likely to come through well.

Hard work, followed by more hard work, will be the order of the day, but genuine effort will be rewarded… even if it takes months for the results to appear. Many people will discover reserves of stamina they never knew they possessed, thanks to the influence of the Ox and perhaps to their surprise, even find themselves enjoying a new sense of satisfaction and pride in their labors.

There will be a great deal to do, that's for sure, but there will be plenty of lighter moments. The Ox loves to be out of doors as much as possible, and prefers to be surrounded by family and close friends rather than navigating crowds of strangers. So, open-air gatherings of loved ones, and the special people in your life, will attract good fortune. Think informal country picnics, beach barbeques, and visits to wildlife parks – anything natural and casual – the Ox never was one for dressing up. And, by happy coincidence, these are exactly the kind of leisure activities we're told will keep us safest as we negotiate the post-Covid months.

Fortunes to be Made

Despite lockdowns around the world, businesses suspended, and talk of recession, the fact is the metal element attracts money, and 2021 will be no exception. The Golden Ox will bring wealth to some quarters.

The changes of last year were all about creating a new landscape, and clearing away outdated methods and industries, to make room for the fresh direction the planet must take. Metal-related businesses such as car manufacturing, IT, and inventions in the fields of domestic appliances, home design, and ecology, will thrive as long as they're embracing the newest technology. Covid-related medical problems will continue to boost pharmaceutical companies. Ox always approves of the patient, methodical way that scientists go about their work, and this year the Golden Ox is likely to shower them with more cash than ever. Expect scientists to come even more to the fore in 2021, along with some genuinely exciting breakthroughs.

Controversy around financial institutions will continue to grow. Huge fortunes will be made but also lost, particularly in cases where there was questionable behavior involved. With big names in industry continuing to crash, it's likely to be the smaller, more adaptable, and down to earth ventures that survive. Ego-driven politicians and captains of industry could be in for a nasty shock in 2021 – particularly as, this year, their own stubbornness could lead to their downfall. And since the metal element is also associated with military might, tensions are unlikely to cool in international hotspots.

The Ox is not greatly interested in travel, so airlines and holiday companies marketing far-flung destinations could continue to struggle. Staycations, particularly those with good 'green' credentials, on the other hand, will boom.

The 1960s was also the decade of space exploration, so it's quite likely we'll see a resurgence of interest in exploring the universe this year. Satellites, discoveries about far-distant planets, and startling UFO activity are likely to make the headlines in 2021. In fact, we could even hear of an alien encounter to rival that of Barney and Betty Hill, that will stun the world.

How the Years Got their Names

According to Chinese folklore, there are many explanations as to why the calendar is divided up the way it is. Perhaps the most popular is the story about the supreme Jade Emperor who lives in heaven. He decided to name each year in honour of a different animal and decreed that a race would be run to decide which animals would be chosen, and the order in which they would appear.

Twelve animals arrived to take part. Actually, in one legend there were 13, and included the cat, at the time a great friend of the rat. But the cat was a sleepy creature and asked the rat to wake him in time for the race and in the excitement (or was it by design?) the rat forgot and dashed off leaving the cat fast asleep. The cat missed the race and missed out on getting a year dedicated to his name. Which is why cats have hated rats ever since.

Anyway, as they approached the finish line, the 12 competitors found a wide river blocking their route. The powerful Ox, a strong swimmer, plunged straight in, but the tiny Rat begged to be carried across on his back. Kindly Ox agreed, but when they reached the opposite bank, the wily Rat scampered down Ox's body, jumped off his head and shot across the finish line in first place. Which is why the Rat is the first animal of the Chinese zodiac, followed by the Ox.

The muscular Tiger, weighed down by his magnificent coat, arrived in third place, followed by the non-swimming Rabbit who'd found some rocks downstream and hopped neatly from one to another to reach dry land.

11

The Emperor was surprised to see the Dragon with his great wings, fly in, in fifth place, instead of the expected first. The Dragon explained that while high up in the sky he saw a village in flames and the people running out of their houses in great distress, so he'd made a detour and employed his rain-making skills (Chinese Dragons can create water as well as fire) to put out the blaze before returning to the race.

In sixth place came the Snake. Clever as the Rat, the Snake had wrapped himself around one of the Horse's hooves and hung on while the Horse swam the river. When the Horse climbed ashore, the Snake slithered off, so startling the Horse that it reared up in alarm, allowing the Snake to slide over the finish line ahead of him.

The Goat, Monkey, and Rooster arrived next at the river. They spotted some driftwood and rope washed up on the shore, so Monkey deftly lashed them together to make a raft and the three of them hopped aboard and floated across. The Goat jumped off first, swiftly followed by Monkey and Rooster. They found they'd beaten the Dog which was unexpected as the Dog was a good swimmer.

It turned out the Dog so enjoyed the water, he'd hung around playing in the shallows emerging only in time to come eleventh. Last of all came the Pig, not the best of swimmers, and further slowed by his decision to pause for a good meal before exerting himself in the current.

And so the wheel of the zodiac was set forevermore, with the Year of the Rat beginning the cycle, followed by the Ox, Tiger, Rabbit, Dragon, Snake, Horse, Goat, Monkey, Rooster, Dog and Pig.

How to Succeed in 2021

So, since 2021 is the Year of the Ox, how will you fare? Does the Ox present your astrological animal with opportunities or challenges? As the fable about how the years got their names shows, every one of the astrological animals is resourceful in its own special way. Faced with the daunting prospect of crossing the river, each successfully made it to the other side, even the creatures that could barely swim.

So whether your year animal gets on easily with the Metal Ox, or whether they have to work at their relationship, you can make 2021 a wonderful year to remember.

Chinese Astrology has been likened to a weather forecast. Once you know whether you need your umbrella or your suntan lotion, you can set out with confidence and enjoy the trip.

Find Your Chinese Astrology Sign

To find your Chinese sign just look up your birth year in the table below.

Important note: if you were born in January or February, check the dates of the New Year very carefully. The Chinese New Year follows the lunar calendar and the beginning and end dates are not fixed, but vary each year. If you were born before mid-February, your animal sign might actually be the sign of the previous year. For example, 1980 was the year of the Monkey but the Chinese New Year began on February 16 so a person born in January or early February 1980 would belong to the year before – the year of the Goat.

And there's more to it than that...

In case you're saying to yourself, but surely, how can every person born in the same 365 days have the same personality(?) – you're quite right. The birth year is only the beginning.

Your birth year reflects the way others see you and your basic characteristics, but your month and time of birth are also ruled by the celestial animals – probably different animals from the one that dominates your birth year. The personalities of these other animals modify and add talents to those you acquired with your birth year creature.

The 1920s

5 February 1924 – 24 January 1925 | RAT

25 January 1925 – 12 February 1926 | OX

13 February 1926 – 1 February 1927 | TIGER

2 February 1927 – 22 January 1928 | RABBIT

23 January 1928 – 9 February 1929 | DRAGON

10 February 1929 – 29 January 1930 | SNAKE

The 1930s

30 January 1930 – 16 February 1931 | HORSE

17 February 1931 – 5 February 1932 | GOAT

6 February 1932 – 25 January 1933 | MONKEY

26 January 1933 – 13 February 1934 | ROOSTER

14 February 1934 – 3 February 1935 | DOG

4 February 1935 – 23 January 1936 | PIG

24 January 1936 – 10 February 1937 | RAT

11 February 1937 – 30 January 1938 | OX

31 January 1938 – 18 February 1939 | TIGER

19 February 1939 – 7 February 1940 | RABBIT

The 1940s

8 February 1940 – 26 January 1941 | DRAGON

27 January 1941 – 14 February 1942 | SNAKE

15 February 1942 – 4 February 1943 | HORSE

5 February 1943 – 24 January 1944 | GOAT

25 January 1944 – 12 February 1945 | MONKEY

13 February 1945 – 1 February 1946 | ROOSTER

2 February 1946 – 21 January 1947 | DOG

22 January 1947 – 9 February 1948 | PIG

10 February 1948 – 28 January 1949 | RAT

29 January 1949 – 16 February 1950 | OX

The 1950s

17 February 1950 – 5 February 1951 | TIGER

6 February 1951 – 26 January 1952 | RABBIT

27 January 1952 – 13 February 1953 | DRAGON

14 February 1953 – 2 February 1954 | SNAKE

3 February 1954 – 23 January 1955 | HORSE

24 January 1955 – 11 February 1956 | GOAT

12 February 1956 – 30 January 1957 | MONKEY

31 January 1957 – 17 February 1958 | ROOSTER

18 February 1958 – 7 February 1959 | DOG

8 February 1959 – 27 January 1960 | PIG

The 1960s

28 January 1960 – 14 February 1961 | RAT

15 February 1961 – 4 February 1962 | OX

5 February 1962 – 24 January 1963 | TIGER

25 January 1963 – 12 February 1964 | RABBIT

13 February 1964 – 1 February 1965 | DRAGON

2 February 1965 – 20 January 1966 | SNAKE

21 January 1966 – 8 February 1967 | HORSE

9 February 1967 – 29 January 1968 | GOAT

30 January 1968 – 16 February 1969 | MONKEY

17 February 1969 – 5 February 1970 | ROOSTER

The 1970s

6 February 1970 – 26 January 1971 | DOG

27 January 1971 – 14 February 1972 | PIG

15 February 1972 – 2 February 1973 | RAT

3 February 1973 – 22 January 1974 | OX

23 January 1974 – 10 February 1975 | TIGER

11 February 1975 – 30 January 1976 | RABBIT

31 January 1976 – 17 February 1977 | DRAGON

18 February 1977 – 6 February 1978 | SNAKE

7 February 1978 – 27 January 1979 | HORSE

28 January 1979 – 15 February 1980 | GOAT

The 1980s

16 February 1980 – 4 February 1981 | MONKEY

5 February 1981 – 24 January 1982 | ROOSTER

25 January 1982 – 12 February 1983 | DOG

13 February 1983 – 1 February 1984 | PIG

2 February 1984 – 19 February 1985 | RAT

20 February 1985 – 8 February 1986 | OX

9 February 1986 – 28 January 1987 | TIGER

29 January 1987 – 16 February 1988 | RABBIT

17 February 1988 – 5 February 1989 | DRAGON

6 February 1989 – 26 January 1990 | SNAKE

The 1990s

27 January 1990 – 14 February 1991 | HORSE

15 February 1991 – 3 February 1992 | GOAT

4 February 1992 – 22 January 1993 | MONKEY

23 January 1993 – 9 February 1994 | ROOSTER

10 February 1994 – 30 January 1995 | DOG

31 January 1995 – 18 February 1996 | PIG

19 February 1996 – 7 February 1997 | RAT

8 February 1997 – 27 January 1998 | OX

28 January 1998 – 5 February 1999 | TIGER

6 February 1999 – 4 February 2000 | RABBIT

The 2000s

5 February 2000 – 23 January 2001 | DRAGON

24 January 2001 – 11 February 2002 | SNAKE

12 February 2002 – 31 January 2003 | HORSE

1 February 2003 – 21 January 2004 | GOAT

22 January 2004 – 8 February 2005 | MONKEY

9 February 2005 – 28 January 2006 | ROOSTER

29 January 2006 – 17 February 2007 | DOG

18 February 2007 – 6 February 2008 | PIG

7 February 2008 – 25 January 2009 | RAT

26 January 2009 – 13 February 2010 | OX

The 2010s

14 February 2010 – 2 February 2011 | TIGER

3 February 2011 – 22 January 2012 | RABBIT

23 January 2012 – 9 February 2013 | DRAGON

10 February 2013 – 30 January 2014 | SNAKE

31 January 2014 – 18 February 2015 | HORSE

19 February 2015 – 7 February 2016 | GOAT

8 February 2016 – 27 January 2017 | MONKEY

28 January 2017 – 15 February 2018 | ROOSTER

16 February 2018 – 4 February 2019 | DOG

5 February 2019 – 24 January 2020 | PIG

The 2020s

25 January 2020 – 11 February 2021 | RAT

12 February 2021 – 31 January 2022 | OX

1 February 2022 – 21 January 2023 | TIGER

22 January 2023 – 9 February 2024 | RABBIT

10 February 2024 – 28 January 2025 | DRAGON

29 January 2025 – 16 February 2026 | SNAKE

17 February 2026 – 5 February 2027 | HORSE

6 February 2027 – 25 January 2028 | GOAT

26 January 2028 – 12 February 2029 | MONKEY

13 February 2029 – 2 February 2030 | ROOSTER

CHAPTER 2: THE OX

Ox Years

25 January 1925 – 12 February 1926

11 February 1937 – 30 January 1938

29 January 1949 – 16 February 1950

15 February 1961 – 4 February 1962

3 February 1973 – 22 January 1974

20 February 1985 – 8 February 1986

8 February 1997 – 27 January 1998

26 January 2009 – 13 February 2010

12 February 2021 – 31 January 2022

Natural Element: Water

Will 2021 be a Golden year for the Ox?

Congratulations, Ox! This year, you are the star of the show. 2021 is your very own year – dedicated to the Ox and the Ox point of view. After more than a decade of putting up with the other signs' efforts at running the planet – some more successful than others in your humble opinion, it has to be said – you've finally got your turn.

The last time you got your cloven hooves on the steering wheel was way back in 2009 when your earthy cousin, the Brown Ox, was in charge. So, it's been a long wait. If you weren't so renowned for your legendary patience, there must have been times when you would have been seething with irritation at the hash some of the less responsible cosmic creatures were making of the task.

But now, at last, you've got the chance to demonstrate how an efficient year should be run. For the next 12 months, the whole world will be dancing to an Ox-like tune. Ox values will rule the globe, and your energy will be irresistible.

Already you're itching to get out there, to calm things down, and to start untangling some of the ridiculous knots people have tied themselves into under the unwise influence of the reckless Rat.

If you're typical of your sign, chances are you've weathered the ups and downs of 2020 pretty well. You and the Rat get along with surprising ease. At a basic level, you both share the element of Water, in the Northern hemisphere you both arrive during the cold months of winter, and – though your personalities are very different – you're both creative types in your own individual ways and can overlook the areas where you disagree.

For these reasons, while some of the astrological animals had a particularly challenging time last year, many Oxen sailed through relatively unscathed. As long as you were an Ox that could work at home or from home, endless weeks of lockdown would be unlikely to phase you. Self-sufficient Ox relishes a period of peace to think things through, formulate a plan, and then quietly put it into action. All in all, for many Oxen, 2020 wasn't too bad. In fact, some Oxen may have secretly enjoyed it.

So, if the year of the Rat wasn't too unsettling for Ox, 2021 is likely to be spectacular for you, right? Well, oddly enough, not necessarily. According to Chinese tradition, the animal that rules the year is not guaranteed a totally trouble-free 12 months.

In decades to come, most Oxen will look back on 2021 and see that the year had a *major* influence on their futures, yet as they're living through it – day to day – the beneficial energies gradually evolving may not be evident.

Then there's the reality of being in charge – of getting the chance to do things your way. Sounds wonderful at first, doesn't it? But with power comes responsibility. And should you make a mistake, there's no one else to blame. What's more, other signs will sense a subtle air of authority about you and look to you for support. Kindly Oxen are always glad to help but also need their own space on a regular basis. At times, many an Ox will be tempted to switch off their phones, retreat indoors, and pretend there's no-one home.

Of course, in many ways, you will be in your element. You're exactly in tune with the mood of the moment. You instinctively know what to do and the best way of doing it. The talents and attitudes you have at your fingertips are the very things most in demand this year. All the best Ox qualities will be on display for 12 whole months, and you'll relish them!

The only slight downside is that it's not just the best Ox qualities that will abound in 2021. Delightful as you are Ox, you have to admit you're not quite perfect, and this year, you could find yourself running into people or situations demonstrating faults you may recognize but deplore. How come there are so many stubborn, inflexible types around all of a sudden, you may find yourself asking. Why do they take so long to complete a task? And should you find yourself goaded beyond reason by their attitudes, why do they have to fly into a rage at the tiniest hint of criticism?

Yes, it's an Ox year, warts and all!

But there will be endless opportunities to make your mark, Ox. Last year, you may have begun a new project or tasted a different way of doing things that proved surprisingly appealing. Now, suddenly, the moment has arrived to build on those foundations and create something splendid. Many Ox will be considering a completely different career or a brand new way of living.

Things that once seemed set in stone are melting away; the barriers are falling and you can sense freedom that didn't seem possible before. Toxic relationships, bullying bosses, a home that never was ideal – suddenly, you realize you don't have to put up with them any longer. Typical Oxen will find an escape route in 2021. Like the border guard who leapt over the Berlin Wall back in 1961, it might not be easy and there may be repercussions, but if you put in the effort, you'll get where you want to go.

And don't forget this is a metal year and metal is very supportive of water creatures. Metal also loves money. Choose your vehicle wisely, and the Golden Ox will propel you towards abundant wealth.

What it Means to Be an Ox

Okay, so hands up everyone who's secretly disappointed to be an astrological Ox?

Sounds a bit bovine and boring, doesn't it? The Ox might lack the glamour of the Tiger or the Dragon. It can't even boast the intriguing notoriety of a sign like the Rat or the Snake. In fact, here in the West, we may not even be entirely sure what an Ox looks like. Some sort of large cow, perhaps?

At first sight, you might be excused for thinking the Ox was dull. Yet, in China, that wasn't the perception at all. There was a very good reason the Ox was so highly placed – at number two – on the zodiac wheel.

The animal was revered as essential to country life. So precious, it was regarded as a gift from the Gods. So special, in fact, it's said that in the past the Chinese didn't eat beef. They couldn't possibly disrespect such an important beast by serving it up for dinner.

So, while the Ox may not seem as exciting as some of the other celestial animals, the sign of the Ox is respected and appreciated.

What the Chinese valued was the phenomenal strength and endurance of the Ox. Get an Ox moving, and it will plod on mile after mile, covering huge distances with apparent ease and without complaint. Without the work of the Ox, many a family would have gone hungry.

People born in the year of the zodiac Ox are believed to be blessed with similar qualities. For this reason, though unflashy and quietly spoken, they often end up being extremely successful in whatever they undertake – from their career to their favorite hobby, or creating a harmonious family that blossoms.

Oxen have a wonderful knack of planning a sensible, logical course to wherever they want to go and then following it, relentlessly, step by step until they get there, no matter what obstacles they encounter en-route. Oxen find it rather puzzling that other people can't seem to adopt the same simple approach. They don't understand why some signs give up before reaching their goal. Why do they waste their time chopping and changing and getting nowhere, wonders the Ox.

Ox patience is legendary. They may not be quick, or nimble, but they realize that slow, steady, consistent effort achieves far more in the long run. And the Ox is only interested in the long haul. At heart, the Ox is serious-minded, and though they enjoy a joke as much as anyone else, they regard frivolity as a pleasant diversion, not an end in itself.

Ox people are usually good-looking in a healthy, wholesome way, but they're not impressed by flashy, passing whims and fashions. Superficial gloss has no appeal. The Ox woman is unlikely to be found rocking extreme, designer clothes or wafting fingers iridescent with the latest nail polish.

Ox tastes tend to be classic and practical. They are instinctively private and hate to draw attention to themselves, yet the Ox is one of the nicest signs. Genuinely honest, kind, and sincere, Ox is ready to help anyone in trouble, happily pitching in to lend a hand without expecting anything in return. Yet, since Ox tends to speak only when they have something to say, other signs can find them difficult to get to know. It's worthwhile making the effort because the Ox will be a loyal friend forever.

What's more, when they do have something to say, Ox views can be surprisingly frank. Just because they are patient and kind, it doesn't mean they can be pushed around. The Ox is self-reliant and makes up its own mind; it's not swayed by the opinions of others. What's more, they can be very stubborn. When the Ox finally makes a decision, it sees no reason to change it.

Ox people are not materialistic. They work hard because the task interests them, or because they can see it needs to be done, and they will keep going until the project is complete. They are the true craftsmen of the zodiac, excelling in working with their hands and they can be unexpectedly artistic and innovative when the occasion demands. As a result, money can accumulate and Ox is not averse to spending it on some creature comforts. The Ox home will be warm and styled for comfort and practicality rather than cutting-edge design. If there's no space for a garden, it's likely to be filled with houseplants too, because Ox has green fingers and needs to see nature close at hand.

Travel and holidays are not top of the Ox agenda; they enjoy their work and their home and are not forever itching to get away. Unlike many signs, they cope with routine very well. And for all their modesty and quiet diligence, there is always something impressive about the Ox. Other signs sense the latent strength and power that lies just below the surface and tend not to impose too much. This is just as well because though the Ox may appear calm, placid, and slow to anger, when they do finally lose their temper, it can be terrifying. What's more, the Ox will never forget an insult and can bear a grudge for years. Ox doesn't stay mad – they get even.

Best Jobs for Ox 2021

Builder

Vet

Market Gardener

Garden Designer

Nurse

Accountant

Potter

Jewellery maker

Plumber

Perfect Partners

Cupid's arrow can strike anywhere at any time, of course, but once the novelty of new romance wears off, some relationships are easier to maintain than others. Here's a guide to the Ox's compatibility with other signs.

Ox with Ox

These two could be very happy together, as long as one of them plucks up the courage to admit they're interested. Sloppy, sentimental romance is not their style and they both share this view so there'll be no misunderstandings around Valentine's Day. They know that still waters run deep and they can enjoy great contentment without showy declarations of love.

Ox with Tiger

Not an easy match. Ox and Tiger could be on different planets. Fiery Tiger doesn't frighten Ox and Tiger may admire Ox's strong, good looks and sincere nature but they both need different things from life. Tiger wants to dash about changing the world for the better, while Ox reckons you get more done by buckling down where you happen to be and attending to the details. Clashes could abound.

Ox with Rabbit

Ox finds Rabbit rather cute and appealing. Whether male or female there's something about Rabbit's inner fluffiness that brings out Ox's highly developed protective instincts. Rabbit meanwhile loves the Ox's reassuring presence and the sense of security Ox provides. These two could get on very well together as long as refined Rabbit can overlook Ox's occasional down-to-earth – Rabbit might say 'coarse' - observations.

Ox with Dragon

Chalk and cheese though this pair may appear to be there's a certain fascination between them. Ox may not approve of Dragon's showy manner but recognizes Dragon's good intentions, while Dragon admires Ox's strength of character and gift for completing tasks. If each could find a way to tolerate the other's wildly different lifestyles, they might be good for each other, but long term, Dragon's hectic pace might wear even the Ox's legendary stamina.

Ox with Snake

Like Ox, the Snake is quietly ambitious and not given to racing around unless it's absolutely necessary. Ox, on the other hand, respects Snake's clever brain and understated elegance. These two could quickly discover how beneficial an alliance between them would be. They're both happy to give the other space when required but also step in with support when needed. This could be a very successful match.

Ox with Horse

Long ago, on many Western farms, Ox was replaced by the Horse and it may be that Ox has never forgotten and never forgiven. At any rate, these two, despite both being big, strong animals, are not usually friends. Horse is too flighty and frivolous to interest Ox for long, while Ox's methodical, careful ways will irritate the Horse. Best not to go there.

Ox with Goat

Though these two share artistic natures even if in the case of the Ox, they're well hidden, deep down, they don't 'get' one another. Ox may be beguiled at first by Goat's friendly, easy-going manner but then disappointed to discover Goat seems to find everyone equally delightful, even those who're plainly unworthy. Goat, on the other hand, can't understand why Ox won't lighten up more. This relationship would require a lot of effort and compromise.

Ox with Monkey

The naughty Monkey scandalizes Ox, but in such an amusing way that Ox can't help laughing. Monkey, on the other hand, is equally amused to find an audience so easy to shock. This unlikely pair enjoy each other's company and get on surprisingly well. Yet, right from the start, it's probably obvious to both that a long term relationship couldn't last. A fun flirtation, though, could be a terrific tonic for them both.

Ox with Rooster

For all its bravado and showing off, the Rooster is a down-to-earth type, drawn to security and accumulating the good things in life – requirements that Ox understands very well and can supply effortlessly. What's more, Ox can't help but admire Rooster's fine feathers and skill at communicating in a crowd – attributes Ox doesn't have and is unlikely to acquire. These two could enjoy a very good partnership.

Ox with Dog

These two ought to get along well as they're both sensible, down to earth, loyal and hardworking and in tune with each other's basic beliefs. And yet, somehow, they don't. Dog has a playful streak and finds this lacking in Ox, while Ox may be baffled by what seems like pointless silliness in Dog. If they can agree to differ, they could make a relationship work.

Ox with Pig

Delightful Pig will catch Ox's eye, and since Pig isn't a constant thrill-seeker, the two of them could enjoy many peaceful evenings together, perhaps over a tasty meal. Yet Pig's spendthrift ways – at least in Ox's eyes, could soon prove very annoying as well as illogical to the Ox, while Pig could find Ox's attitude judgmental and upsetting. Not ideal for the long term.

Ox with Rat

Oddly enough, this combination can be surprisingly successful. Frenetic Rat and calm Ox may seem to be opposites, but in fact Rat can find Ox's laid-back approach strangely soothing. Ox is not interested in competing with Rat and will patiently put up with Rat's scurrying after new schemes. As long as Rat doesn't get bored and generates enough excitement in other areas of life, this relationship could be very contented.

Ox Love 2021 Style

There's no avoiding it, Ox. This year you're going to be in demand. Other signs would kill for the kind of popularity on offer to you in 2021, but the modest Ox can be surprisingly bashful when it comes to romance. This year, you could find all the attention a bit overwhelming.

The typical Ox prefers quality to quantity when it comes to partners. Ox prefers to gaze longingly from afar at some super-fit apparition, discreetly learning as much as possible about the beloved before making a move. Well, that tactic might prove a bit difficult this year. The powerful energy exuded by a great big Golden Ox in the room is unlikely to go unnoticed.

The ruler of the year is always going to radiate a magnetic appeal. Potential loves can't help but be drawn towards the dominant animal, and this year that's you, Ox. Get used to it!

Single Oxen will have their pick of partners, and Oxen already in relationships will struggle to reassure their other halves they're not flirting. 2021 will be a testing time for relationships that are at all rocky. In fact, many an Ox could find themselves finally walking away from a liaison that was maybe never ideal, or perhaps was good a while ago but has recently run out of road.

The good news is that solid, happy partnerships are set to flourish, and single or newly-single Oxen will have plenty of choice before committing themselves again.

Secrets of Success in 2021

The truth is, you can't help but be a success in 2021, Ox, because this is *your* year and *your* talents are in demand. The only thing that could hold you back is you, yourself. You have all the gifts you need, plus the phenomenal stamina to put them to good use in awesome amounts.

Trouble is, it's no use producing mountains of excellent work if no one knows you've done it, or worse, if someone else is trying to claim the praise. Self-promotion has never been your thing, Ox. You don't like to brag, which is admirable, but you can take modesty too far. Your abilities are much more likely to be noticed if you get out there and show them off.

It's not easy for you, Ox, to come over all extrovert, but if you can overcome your reticence and draw attention to your skills, big-time, you'll be amazed at the results. Fame and fortune could be yours.

The other thing to watch out for is that temper of yours and the tendency to suddenly get obstinate over a small detail. Some would be surprised to learn that quiet, sensible Ox has a temper. You're normally so laid-back. This is true. But push an Ox too far, and the sudden explosion of rage could make the sky fall in.

Similarly, there's that stubborn streak. Usually, the Ox is the most amenable and reasonable of creatures, but try to hurry Ox along – try to force the pace – and the result is stress. When that happens, Ox's peculiar way of dealing with tension is to get fixated on one tiny, seemingly unimportant issue, and refuse to budge. Many a deal has been unexpectedly lost because of Ox's objection to the color of the ink to be used on the contract, or the time of day for a meeting to be held.

Get a grip Ox, keep cool, and 2021 will be one of your greatest years.

The Ox Year At a glance

January – Get plenty of rest. Gather your energy for next month.

February – New Year arrives. Crack open the champagne. This is your Year, Ox.

March – You're loving getting organized. Things may be quiet, but your plans are progressing.

April – A showy character at work may be annoying, but keep calm. They could be surprisingly helpful in months to come.

May – A friend or colleague has an intriguing idea. Your input could work wonders.

June – A spiteful individual could cause friction in a relationship. Watch out.

July – Romance could still be tricky. Misunderstandings abound. Tact and diplomacy could save the day.

August – Phew, looks like you've smoothed things over. This would be a good month for some fun or a long holiday.

September – Someone needs a helping hand. Your efforts will be rewarded.

October – Time to settle down and put in some serious work. Your plans are coming together. Get ready for the final push.

November – Unexpected expenses may irritate. Count to ten and don't over-react. You can sort this.

December – Just when the pace is hotting up, everyone wants to stop and party. Take a break, Ox. Everything's going well. Enjoy yourself.

Lucky colors for 2021: Green, yellow, white

Lucky numbers: 1, 4

CHAPTER 3: THE TIGER

Tiger Years

13 February 1926 – 1 February 1927

31 January 1938 – 18 February 1939

17 February 1950 – 5 February 1951

5 February 1962 – 24 January 1963

23 January 1974 – 10 February 1975

9 February 1986 – 28 January 1987

28 January 1998 – 5 February 1999

14 February 2010 – 2 February 2011

1 February 2022 – 21 January 2023

Natural Element: Wood

Will 2021 be a Golden Year for the Tiger?

Well, Tiger, chances are 2020 didn't pan out quite the way you expected. Many a Tiger hoped to make changes last year and go off-grid in some way. And, in fact, you did – though what you had in mind was probably more like a trip to the remoter regions of the Amazon, instead of months holed up in your bedroom, interspersed with prowls around the local park.

Yet, in a strange way, the upheavals of last year have produced the same affect you'd hoped to achieve with a more exciting interlude. The break from normality has allowed you to expand your imagination and get in touch with your intuition. You may not realize it yet, but you now stand aligned to the very place where you *need to be* for your next step.

And 2021 is the year you'll start to see real progress towards an important new goal. If you were annoyed that the circumstances of the previous months forced you to put ambitious plans on ice – don't be. Either those plans were unwise, or they needed more thought and refinement. You are now ready to create something new or improve on those existing ideas and put them into practice in a better form. The year of the Golden Ox is the perfect time to do it.

To be honest, the dashing Tiger and the slow-moving Ox are not the most natural comrades. They can quite easily rub each other up the wrong way. Yet, the Ox always respects hard work and discipline, and after a long spell of enforced idleness, normally impetuous Tiger is keen to get stuck in and labor conscientiously to make up for lost time. For once, Tiger, the two of you are in sync, and Ox will be right behind your serious efforts, cheering you on.

What's more, although this is a metal year, the Ox is at heart a water creature while the Tiger is regarded as belonging to the Wood family. Water is believed to be beneficial to wood – since all trees and plants depend on water in order to grow – so the Tiger can expect to enjoy a lot of help this year. Some of it from quite unexpected quarters.

Also, since the Ox loves the great outdoors, nature, and anything to do with wildlife, idealistic Tigers who decide to channel their altruistic instincts into environmental schemes will get a major boost. If you want to save the rain forest, Tiger, rid the world of plastic pollution, or take up a green career, you will succeed with ease.

Tigers tend to be highly individual personalities, and for that reason, they are often self-employed – or would like to be. Taking orders doesn't come naturally to the rebellious Tiger, and many big cats have an uneasy relationship with their boss. Deep down, the boss is likely to be slightly scared of the Tiger underling, which doesn't help the situation.

It's often best all-round when the Tiger decides to go it alone. And surprisingly, the Ox understands this completely. Oxen also prefer to work unencumbered, though for different reasons. Ox doesn't much care who's in charge – it's the task in hand that's important – and most Oxen find they can get more done without a colleague constantly chattering in their ear and forever wondering if they'd like a cup of tea.

Bearing this in mind, despite the uncertain times, many Tigers will be inspired to strike out alone this year or start their own business. Despite the horrified warnings of friends and families, this type of venture is likely to succeed as long as the Tiger is prepared to put in months of relentless hard work. Remember those bids for freedom we saw in 1961? You *can* break away in an Ox year – as long as you're willing to pay the price.

If you're a typical Tiger, money is not a major motivator. You've never been the materialistic type. You're not against splashing the cash, of course, and would rather have a healthy bank balance than a maxed-out credit card, but – in truth – you'd prefer to spend your time doing something fascinating rather than slaving at a soul-destroying job that pays well. Fortunately, as this is a metal year and metal attracts money, you should find that when you need it, the cash you require will turn up. That's not to say it's fine to take out big loans or run up your overdraft – the thrifty Ox deplores risky behavior especially with finances – but when funds are low, a timely offer of overtime, an increase in salary, or a windfall of some sort is likely to boost the Tiger coffers.

Tigers love to travel, and the restrictions of last year will have been particularly frustrating. Chances are most people will still be encouraged to stay closer to home in 2021 – especially as the Ox is not renowned for desiring frequent changes of scene. Yet, one sign that's likely to find a way to sidestep stifling rules is yours, Tiger. Somehow, you'll find a way to combine business with pleasure. You might even get that trip to the rainforest after all.

What it Means to Be a Tiger

It's a wonderful thing to be a Tiger. Who could not be impressed with the great cat's magnificent striped coat, lithe yet powerful body, and arrogant, swaggering stride? We're all in awe of the Tiger – as well as being pretty scared, too.

In China, the sign is regarded as fortunate and noble. Fortunate because – let's face it – the Tiger owns the jungle and patrols his territory with savage grace; noble because it's believed the Tiger only kills when it's hungry or threatened. (Which may or may not be strictly true.)

Yet the zodiac Tiger is also a contrary creature. You never know quite where you are with the typical Tiger. With a coat that's neither black nor orange – neither light nor dark – Tigers have two sides to their characters and can switch moods in an instant.

What's more, that striped pelt provides such perfect camouflage in the jungle; Tiger can melt into the shadows and become completely invisible, only to reappear without warning when least expected, to devastating effect.

Other signs instinctively know never to underestimate the Tiger.

Perhaps unsurprisingly, people born under this sign tend to attract good luck. They throw themselves into risky situations and escape unscathed, where others would come badly unstuck.

Tigers are fearless and restless. They like to be on the move and get bored easily. Wonderfully good-looking, Tigers tend to shine in company, and enjoy being surrounded by admirers, as they usually are. While perfectly happy in their own company and not craving attention, Tigers are confident and unfazed by a crowd. They take it as quite natural that other signs seek them out and want to hear their opinions.

The Tiger has a magnetic personality and can be highly entertaining, but they're also surprisingly moody – laughing and joking one minute, then flying into a rage over almost nothing the next. Despite this, the Tiger is very idealistic. Tiger can see what's wrong with the world and wants to put it right. What's more, courageous Tiger is quite prepared to get out there and put the necessary changes into action.

This is the sign of the daring revolutionary. The trouble is, Tigers can become so accustomed to getting away with audacious acts, they forget that – deep down – they're big cats and cats are said to have only nine lives. Push their luck too far, and sooner or later, Tiger can find it runs out.

Sporty and athletic, Tigers love to travel; when they're young, the typical Tiger is likely to want to be off to see the world. Even older Tigers insist on regular holidays and would happily take a sabbatical or 'adult gap year' if possible. Luxury travel or budget breaks, they don't really care as long as they're going somewhere different. They don't even mind going on their own if necessary, as they're independent and self-assured; they are confident they'll find an interesting companion from time to time, along the way, if they need one.

Far too individual to be slaves to fashion, Tigers of both sexes still manage to look stylish and original in a pared-down, sleek sort of way. They can't be bothered with fiddly, fussy details, and they don't need to be because their natural features attract attention effortlessly. Similarly, the Tiger's home is attractive and unusual: full of intriguing objects and trophies that Tiger has collected during their adventures.

At work, if they manage to avoid quarrelling with the boss and walking out – a strong possibility as Tigers hate to be told what to do – Tigers tend to rise to the top of whatever field they happen to be in. But contradictory to the end, the Tiger is just as likely to reach the peak of their profession and then resign to try something new. In business, the Tiger can be creative, innovative, and utterly ruthless to competitors.

Best Jobs for Tiger in 2021

Revolutionary

Environmentalist

Social Worker

Scientist

Documentary Maker

Perfect Partners

Cupid's arrow can strike anywhere at any time, of course, but once the novelty of new romance wears off, some relationships are easier to maintain than others. Here's a guide to the Tiger's compatibility with other signs.

Tiger with Tiger

The attraction between these two beautiful people is powerful. They understand each other so well, it's almost like looking in a mirror. They both like to walk on the wild side and will enjoy some exciting adventures together, but their moody interludes could lead to fierce quarrels. This match could be compulsive but stormy.

Tiger with Rabbit

Surprisingly, the Rabbit is not intimidated by Tiger's dangerous aura, and this attitude immediately appeals to Tiger who enjoys a challenge. Rabbit's calm presence and clever way with words keeps Tiger interested, while Rabbit finds Tiger's adventurous tales entertaining. With care, these two could get on well together for years.

Tiger with Dragon

The two biggest personalities in the zodiac would seem bound to clash. After all, these larger than life characters share so many similarities there's a danger they'd compete. Yet a relationship between the Tiger and Dragon often works very well. They understand each other's impulsive natures, but they're also different enough to supply the support the other needs. They'd make a formidable power couple.

Tiger with Snake

Not the best of romances. These two are so fundamentally different that any initial attraction is unlikely to last. Snake likes to bask and conserve energy while Tiger wants to leap right in and race about. Tiger takes in the big picture in a glance and is off to the next challenge while Snake likes to pause, delve beneath the surface, and consider. It wouldn't take long before these two annoy each other.

Tiger with Horse

This athletic pair get on pretty well. They both like physical pursuits, testing their strength out of doors or just enjoying the feel of the wind in their hair and the ground under their feet. True, Horse may not quite understand Tiger's plans for world domination, but it doesn't really matter. Horse is happy to be loyal to such a charismatic partner. As they're both moody, there could be rows, but making up is exciting.

Tiger with Goat

Tiger and Goat don't have a lot in common. While their aims and temperaments are quite different, they are both sociable creatures, and Goat wouldn't mind Tiger attracting all the attention when they're out together. Tiger, in return, would appreciate Goat's lack of jealousy and generosity of spirit. Yet, long-term, they're likely to drift apart as they follow their different interests.

Tiger with Monkey

Tiger can't help being intrigued by sparkling Monkey and Monkey is flattered by such interest. Who wouldn't enjoy being admired by such a fabulous creature? But irrepressible Monkey just can't help teasing and being teased is not a sensation Tiger is familiar with, nor appreciates. Unless the attraction is very strong, these two will wind each other up until they can bear it no longer and part.

Tiger with Rooster

The only feathered creature in the zodiac, the opulence and novelty of Rooster's appearance will draw Tiger like a magnet. What's more, deep down they are both quite serious-minded types so, on one level, they'll have much to share. Yet, despite this, they're not really on the same wavelength, and misunderstandings will keep recurring. Could be hard work.

Tiger with Dog

While not exactly opposites, these two are different enough to intrigue each other yet similar enough in basic outlook to get on well. Both Tiger and Dog are idealistic and uninterested in material gain yet where Dog can be nervous, Tiger's bold; and where Tiger attracts controversy, Dog will be loyal. This partnership could be lasting and valuable.

Tiger with Pig

Carefree Pig will love to bask in Tiger's impressive aura, while Tiger will feel good about protecting this charming but unworldly creature. They enjoy each other's company and Tiger, so focused on lofty matters will find Pig's compulsive shopping too trivial to worry about. This couple could do well together as long as Pig's fondness for cozy nights in doesn't make Tiger feel trapped.

Tiger with Rat

Sleek and clever Rat can easily attract Tiger's attention because the intelligent Tiger loves witty conversation. Yet these two are not natural partners. Tiger's not interested in Rat's latest bargain and has no wish to talk about it while Rat doesn't share Tiger's passion for changing the world. Still, if they can agree to step back and not get in each other's way, they could reach a good understanding.

Tiger with Ox

Not an easy match. Ox and Tiger could be on different planets. Fiery Tiger doesn't frighten Ox, and Tiger may admire Ox's strong, good looks and sincere nature, but they both need different things from life. Tiger wants to dash about creating big changes, while Ox reckons you get more done by buckling down where you happen to be and attending to the details. Clashes could abound.

Tiger Love 2021 Style

You've never been short of admirers, Tiger, even if half the time you scarcely notice them. Though they come in all shapes and sizes, Tigers share natural good looks and an unconscious feline grace. You turn heads wherever you go, and this has probably been happening for so long you don't even realize the effect you have.

Deep down, you tend to take it all for granted. This year, though, things could be a little different. You're still as attractive as ever, don't worry, but now for some reason, the settled, more placid vibes of the Ox are getting to you. Where once Tiger could be relied upon to *love 'em and leave 'em'*, to point out at frequent intervals how you hate to be tied down, in 2021 you feel a subtle shift.

This could be the year single Tigers start to consider quite seriously how nice it might be to have a permanent partner. And with travel more limited than usual, there's finally time to stay in one place long enough to develop promising relationships.

Your soulmate could very well emerge this year, Tiger, and when they do, you'll be amazed how different they make you feel. Becoming tied down doesn't seem to sound nearly as unwelcome as you thought. In fact, it could even appear quite appealing. Many a Tiger will be looking at wedding rings this year.

Attached Tigers could find themselves viewing their partner with fresh eyes. In the past, if you're typical of your sign, you've probably been guilty of failing to pay them enough attention or sparing them much of your precious time. In 2021, it suddenly dawns on you that you'd mind quite a lot if they got tired of waiting. Ok, so the Tiger is unlikely to change its stripes, but this year you could decide to make much more *effort*. You'll be amazed at the results. With a little thought and consideration, you can relaunch the relationship and make it better than it's ever been.

Secrets of Success

You're on the launch pad, Tiger, and the new future you want to create is within sight. The most important thing to remember to avoid jinxing your good fortune is to try not to annoy the Ox. In practical terms, that involves refraining from the type of behavior that sets Ox's teeth on edge.

Rushing around, starting numerous new projects, then skipping off to distant pastures without completing them is a definite no-no. As is skimming over the details, refusing to read the small print, failing to get to grips with your accounts, and insisting on doing everything at 100 miles an hour.

Drumming your fingers, tapping your feet, or rolling your eyes when dealing with a slower moving person – even when they don't catch you doing it – will also bring on bad karma. And if you have a boss, so will picking a fight with them or deliberately sabotaging their stupid instructions.

Just pin a sweet smile to your face at all times, bite your tongue when provoked, and work as hard as humanly possible at your chosen project, and this year, you can't fail, Tiger.

The Tiger Year at a Glance

January – Good news arrives as the old Rat year fades out, and you're feeling positive.

February – A charity fires your imagination, and you're inspired to take part or lend a hand.

March – Someone's giving you mixed messages either at work or in a relationship. Logic won't help with this one. Trust your gut instinct.

April – Tact and diplomacy are called for. An authority figure is annoying. No harm is intended. You can handle them.

May – Domestic bliss is brewing. Whatever you've been doing on the home front is working wonders. Keep doing what you're doing!

June – Even if you don't think of yourself as creative, you've got hidden talents. They're emerging this month.

July – Tigers have boundless energy, but even big cats need some downtime. Treat yourself to some R&R.

August – It's party month somewhere near you, Tiger. Accept all invitations – socially distanced, of course.

September – Baby news surrounds you this month. Is there a new cub in the family?

October – Finances are on the up. Don't go crazy, but you can afford to spoil yourself now.

November – Irritable people keep crossing your path. They can't help it. Be patient – you're a winner.

December – Christmas shopping tends to stress you, Tiger, if you can be bothered at all that is. Avoid the hassle, relax, and enjoy the celebrations. You've come a long way.

Lucky colors for 2021: Blue, Green, White

Lucky numbers for 2021: 3, 7

CHAPTER 4: THE RABBIT

Rabbit Years

2 February 1927 – 22 January 1928

19 February 1939 – 7 February 1940

6 February 1951 – 26 January 1952

25 January 1963 – 12 February 1964

11 February 1975 – 30 January 1976

29 January 1987 – 16 February 1988

6 February 1999 – 4 February 2000

3 February 2011 – 22 January 2012

22 January 2023 – 9 February 2024

Natural Element: Wood

Will 2021 be a Golden Year for the Rabbit?

Good news, Rabbit. It looks like you're going to enjoy 2021 much more than 2020! If you're typical of your sign, chances are that last year wasn't too bad for you in practical terms, but it probably didn't feel like that at the time.

The whole world had troubles in the recently departed Year of the Rat, of course, but for you, Rabbit, the upheavals were particularly unsettling because you're the sensitive type. You're highly intuitive too, so even if nothing appears to be going wrong on the surface, those acute little whiskers and super-sharp ears are always primed and scanning the horizon, ready to detect the tiniest trace of trouble on the wind. And, of course, there were plenty of worrying vibes to pick up last year, which didn't help. Even if they weren't winging their way to Rabbit's abode, they were still a source of stress to the apprehensive bunny.

It also didn't help that last year was a metal year – the type of year that always makes Rabbits a bit jumpy. The fact that metal years also tend to bring cash showering down onto most suspicious bobtails doesn't compensate as far as many Rabbits are concerned. This is because, as well as being associated with money, metal is also linked to sharp cutting instruments and weapons – all of which make peaceable Rabbits distinctly nervous. No matter how well things appear to be going, Rabbit can't escape the feeling, deep down, that some horrible threat might be lurking.

So, it might not please you to learn that 2021 is also a metal year. But hang on a minute, Rabbit, before you bolt to your burrow for the duration. This year there's no need to panic. This is a different kind of metal altogether. The metal associated with the Golden Ox comes in a much milder form. The ferocious energy that screeched through 2020 like a chainsaw has blown itself out, to be replaced by metal in a gentler shape – the kind associated with candlesticks and jewelry, ornamental gates and useful, unthreatening household items.

This is the kind of metal you can cope with Rabbit, the kind that is not too scary and which has the added advantage of boosting your bank balance.

The other good news is that this is the Year of the Ox, and the Ox brings a wonderful feeling of stability. Rabbits thrive on stability, and after the unpredictable events of last year, this calming influence is even more welcome than usual.

As you emerge cautiously into 2021 to take stock, you can look around and possibly surprise yourself, Rabbit. With all the fire-fighting many Rabbits felt obliged to do last year, you probably didn't notice something that was starting to come together and grow in a very pleasing way. Some project you were involved with, or some idea that captured your imagination, has begun to take on a life of its own. It's early days yet, but if you nurture this little seedling, it has the potential to develop into something that will bring you great success.

This may not be the year you feel inclined to change jobs or take big risks with your finances, Rabbit, unless there really is no option. The Golden Ox will instead offer you the chance to dig deep into your talents, hone your gifts, and accomplish more than you ever dreamed possible. Your efforts will not go unrewarded either.

The Ox and the Rabbit get along very well together. While Rabbit admires the Ox strength and tenacity, the Ox is fascinated by tiny Rabbit's delicacy and precision. Ox feels quite protective of the Rabbit. What's more, the Ox is a water creature while the Rabbit is from the wood family and, traditionally, water nurtures wood – since all plant life depends on water to survive. For these reasons, this year you'll get all the help you need Rabbit. Supporters are on hand to come to your aid in every area of life. All you'll have to do is ask. Sometimes you won't even have to do that. Should difficulties arise, chances are a stranger will pass by – at just the right moment – to sort the problem or provide the expertise you require.

With all the enforced time at home, last year, you'd think many Rabbits would be only too glad to rush outside and head for the hills. Yet, oddly, typical Rabbits have found themselves becoming even more interested in their surroundings. Some might be daydreaming about building their own property, others making plans for major improvements, or moving elsewhere altogether, or possibly getting another place in the country even if it's only a tent. With the extra cash coming your way this year, Rabbit, you can turn these dreams into reality.

Family is going to play a big part in your plans in 2021, Rabbit. In fact, many Rabbits may be considering reorganizing their careers to spend more time with loved ones. If so, this would be the perfect time to retrain or begin a course of study for new qualifications. As long as you work hard, the studious Ox will be on hand to push success your way.

What it Means to Be a Rabbit

We all love Rabbits, don't we? After the possibly dull Ox and terrifying Tiger, the soft and pretty Rabbit seems like a welcome relief. We can all relate to the Rabbit. Big brown eyes, powder puff-tail, cute little quivering nose, and an endearing way of hopping neatly around – nobody could take offence at the Rabbit.

In fact, nobody could feel threatened by the Rabbit in any way unless they happen to be a carrot, or a salad vegetable.

Yet, in the West, not all zodiac Rabbits are proud of their sign. They believe it suggests vulnerability and lack of drive. In the East, however, the Rabbit is appreciated for some very important qualities.

Like the Rat, Rabbits are brilliant survivors; they thrive and colonize in all manner of difficult terrains; but, unlike the Rat, they manage to do this – mostly – without enraging or disgusting anyone, bar a few irritated farmers.

For all their cuddly looks, these are tough little creatures, frequently under-estimated. It's no accident that in the Chinese calendar, the defenseless, non-swimming Rabbit still manages to cross the river in fourth place, way ahead of stronger, abler creatures with seemingly much more going for them.

People born under this sign are never flashy or loud. Enter a crowded room, and the Rabbit wouldn't be the first person you notice. Yet, after a while, a stylish, immaculately-turned-out character would draw your eye. Classy and understated with perfect hair and graceful gestures – the typical Rabbit. This effortlessly polished aura is a gift. A Rabbit can emerge soaked to the skin from a rainstorm in a muddy field and within minutes appear clean, unruffled, and coordinated. Even Rabbits don't know how they do it. They're not even aware they *are* doing it.

Rabbits are refined with cultured tastes. They love beautiful things and art of all kinds, and hate to be surrounded by untidiness and disorder. Harmony is very important to the Rabbit – both visually and emotionally. People born in Rabbit years are sensitive in every way. They hate loud noises, loud voices, heavy traffic, and general ugliness. Quarrels can actually make them ill.

Yet this loathing of discord doesn't mean the Rabbit retires from the world. Rabbits somehow manage to end up near the center of the action and tend to walk away with what they want, without appearing to have made any visible effort to get it.

Softly-spoken Rabbits are natural diplomats. Discreet and tactful, they can always find the right words, the perfect solutions to keep everybody happy. In fact, their powers of persuasion are so sophisticated that people usually do what Rabbit wants in the belief it's their own idea. This approach is so successful that Rabbit can't understand why other signs resort to argument and challenge, when so much more can be achieved through quiet conversation and compromise.

Rabbits tend to be brilliant strategists. When other egos get too distracted, jockeying for position and trying to be in charge for the task in hand, Rabbit deftly assesses the situation and has a plan worked out before the others have even agreed an agenda. Outwardly modest, Rabbits rarely admit to being ambitious, so they often end up being underestimated. Yet, privately, Rabbits can be single-minded and determined; even ruthless at times. These qualities, combined with their diplomatic skills and calm efficiency, seem to propel them smoothly to the top of whatever profession they've chosen.

Rabbits love their homes, which naturally are as beautiful and harmonious as they are. Home is a sanctuary and Rabbits take a lot of pleasure in choosing just the right pieces and décor to make their special place perfect, but in a comfortable way. Tidiness comes easily to them, and they can bring order to chaos quickly and neatly with the minimum of fuss. They enjoy entertaining – preferably small, informal gatherings of good friends – and they make wonderful hosts. Since they are such agreeable types, they're popular with everyone and a Rabbit's invitation to dinner is accepted with eagerness.

When life is calm and secure, the Rabbit is perfectly happy to stay in one place. These types are not desperate for novelty though they do enjoy a relaxing holiday. Extreme sports are unlikely to appeal, but gentle exercise in beautiful surroundings soothes their nerves, and if they can take in an art gallery or a historic church followed by a delicious meal, they'd be truly contented bunnies.

Best Jobs for Rabbit 2021

Fashion model

Psychiatrist

Diplomat

Business Consultant

Cosmetic Dentist

Interior Designer

Hairstylist

Estate Agent

Personal Shopper

Perfect Partners

Cupid's arrow can strike anywhere at any time, of course, but once the novelty of new romance wears off, some relationships are easier to maintain than others. Here's a guide to the Rabbit's compatibility with other signs.

Rabbit with Rabbit

These two gorgeous creatures look like they're made for each other. Their relationship will always be calm, peaceful, and unruffled and it goes without saying that their home could grace a glossy magazine. Yet though they never argue, the willingness of both partners to compromise could end up with neither ever quite doing what they want. Ultimately, they may find the spark goes out.

Rabbit with Dragon

Dragon is such a larger than life character Rabbit could feel overwhelmed at times. Also, the Dragon can be rather noisy and over-dramatic which would get on Rabbit's nerves. Yet they each admire the other's good points. If they could live next door to each other instead of under the same roof, a long-term relationship might work.

Rabbit with Snake

This subtle pair could make a good combination. They both understand the value of working behind the scenes and neither has any desire to wear themselves out on endless adventures. They share a love of art, fine things, and quiet pleasures, and they both enjoy an orderly home. These two could settle down very happily together.

Rabbit with Horse

This could be tricky. It's fairly unlikely that Horse and Rabbit would ever end up on a date but if they did, and there was a strong attraction, it could lead to a love/hate relationship. Rabbit's neat and tidy ways would enrage Horse and Horse's unpredictable moods and over-the-top reactions would annoy Rabbit. Soon, Horse is likely to bolt for the hills or Rabbit retreat to its burrow.

Rabbit with Goat

Happy-go-lucky Goat is very appealing to Rabbit, particularly as deep down Rabbit is a bit of a worrier. They're both sociable without needing to be the center of attention and would be happy to people-watch for hours and then cheerfully compare notes afterwards. Goat is tolerant of Rabbit's need for some regular alone time to recharge too, so this couple could be a successful match.

Rabbit with Monkey

Mercurial Monkey doesn't really 'get' Rabbit. The Monkey can appreciate how well Rabbit operates and sees this approach gets good results, but it's all too picky and slow for Monkey. Rabbit, on the other hand, is amused by Monkey's quick wit and clever ways but deplores Monkey's slapdash, sometimes devious tactics. Very unlikely to work out.

Rabbit with Rooster

Another difficult match. However unfair it seems, Rooster comes over as loud, boastful, and uncouth to Rabbit while Rabbit appears dull, staid, and insufficiently admiring of Rooster's fine feathers to appeal to Rooster. These two just can't see below the surface of the other, and it would be surprising if they ended up together. Only to be considered by the very determined.

Rabbit with Dog

Despite the fact that in the outside world Rabbit could easily end up as Dog's dinner, the astrological pair get on surprisingly well. Dog appreciates Rabbit's careful, efficient ways and soft voice, while Rabbit admires Dog's energy and good intentions. Dog's lack of interest in the finer points of interior design might try Rabbit's patience, but with a little work these two could reach an understanding.

Rabbit with Pig

Pig is not quite as interested in fine dining as Rabbit being as happy to scoff a burger as a Cordon Bleu creation, but their shared love of the good things in life makes these two happy companions. Once again, Pig's spending habits might irritate Rabbit, but not too much as Rabbit is quite willing to splurge on lovely things for the home. A relationship would work well.

Rabbit with Rat

Rat finds Rabbit intriguing. Here is an attractive, stylish creature that doesn't feel the need to be pushy or take center stage yet somehow manages to be at the heart of things, while Rabbit is flattered and entertained by witty Rat's attention. These two respect each other but long-term, Rat could be too overpowering unless they both agree to give each other space.

Rabbit with Ox

Ox finds Rabbit rather cute and appealing. Whether male or female there's something about Rabbit's inner fluffiness that brings out Ox's highly-developed protective instincts. Rabbit meanwhile loves the Ox's reassuring presence, and the sense of security Ox provides. These two could get on very well together as long as refined Rabbit can overlook Ox's occasional down-to-earth – Rabbit might say 'coarse' – observations.

Rabbit with Tiger

Surprisingly the Rabbit is not intimidated by Tiger's dangerous aura and this attitude immediately appeals to Tiger who enjoys a challenge. Rabbit's calm presence and clever way with words keeps Tiger interested, while Rabbit finds Tiger's adventurous tales entertaining. With care, these two could get on well together for years.

Rabbit Love 2021 Style

Last year was all set to be particularly frisky for the quietly flirtatious Rabbit – but then COVID swept in, and all that social distancing put paid to many a promising romance.

The other signs still see you as smoking-hot, Rabbit, but possibly, as the year begins, you find all that stress of the last 12 months has drained your enthusiasm. Well, don't worry about it. As the weeks go by and you find yourself relaxing, springtime will work its usual magic. Single Rabbits are in for a fun-filled 2021 as fellow Rabbits – plus most of the other signs – will be eager to make up for lost time. You'll be hopping from partner to partner in a happy, light-hearted way.

Attached Rabbits could find themselves seriously considering expanding the family, under the influence of the traditional, dynastically-inclined Ox. This may well involve expanding the family homestead, too, to make room for new arrivals. You can look forward to long, delightful evenings with your partner making plans and then putting them into action.

Secret of Success in 2021

You have, before you, all you need for success in 2021, Rabbit – although you may not recognize it at first. Something begun last year, or even the year before, is quietly gathering pace. All it needs is a little more care and attention to polish it into a spectacular opportunity for you.

It may, at this stage, be little more than an idea that occurred to you a while ago and which has been silently germinating at the back of your mind ever since. Now is the time to bring it to the surface, and start putting it into action.

Above all, you have to wrench yourself out of the past. Most Rabbits are inclined to be cautious. This is not a bad thing in itself, and it's far better to be careful than reckless. Yet the worries of 2020 have had a detrimental effect on the typical Rabbit's confidence, and some have become almost too frightened to make a move.

While it's not a good idea to go overboard, you can afford to be a little bolder in 2021, Rabbit. Try something different, accept those unusual invitations. Talk to people you wouldn't normally meet, and really listen to what they have to say. By the time the Golden Ox is heading away for another 60 years, you may be amazed and delighted at how far you've come.

The Rabbit Year at a Glance

January – As last year's Rat is preparing to leave to make way for the brand new Ox, you suddenly realize how much repair work is needed. Get ready to roll up your sleeves.

February – There aren't enough hours in the day, but social life is picking up. Make time for some fun.

March – Spring is in the air, and someone's got their eye on you. If you're in a relationship, take care!

April – Confidence is growing and the better you feel, the more you want to do. Don't overload yourself, though. There are many months of the year left.

May – The boss has noticed your efforts, and you could be flavor of the month right now. Keep that modest smile in place. Don't make your colleagues jealous.

June – Midsummer and hours of sun suit you, Rabbit. You're feeling good. This could be an excellent time to enjoy a holiday.

July – The warm weather is relaxing you so much you're tempted to spend – and spend lavishly. You've got good taste Rabbit but is this really necessary? Think before you splurge.

August – You've succeeded in calming the stress, but it might be better to avoid the crowds in peak holiday season. Keep cool, and take another break when it's quieter.

September – The pace quickens, and the tasks are building up. Don't expect to do it all on your own Rabbit – delegate.

October – Good news on the family front makes you smile, and a pay rise could be on the way.

November – As the nights draw in, avoid overwork. You can afford to slow down now and take stock of all you've achieved so far.

December – All around you, people are hoping to party. You're not too bothered. It's good to look forward to some calm family time.

Lucky colors for 2021: Blue, white, orange

Lucky numbers for 2021: 4, 6

CHAPTER 5: THE DRAGON

Dragon Years

23 January 1928 – 9 February 1929

8 February 1940 – 26 January 1941

27 January 1952 – 13 February 1953

13 February 1964 – 1 February 1965

31 January 1976 – 17 February 1977

17 February 1988 – 5 February 1989

5 February 2000 – 23 January 2001

23 January 2012 – 9 February 2013

10 February 2024 – 28 January 2025

Natural Element: Wood

Will 2021 be a Golden Year for the Dragon?

If you've entered 2021 with mixed feelings, Dragon, no one could blame you. There you were last year, all fired up and ready to storm through the Year of the Rat in a blaze of glory, when along came the great lockdown and suddenly your plans crashed to earth like damp fireworks in a downpour.

It should have been your year, Dragon, yet somehow it wasn't. So now you're probably feeling a bit cheated. A bit rebellious even. Yet the odd thing is, for many Dragons, it *was* your year – you're just still standing too close to see it yet. The Rat brought you opportunities, but they didn't come in the form you expected. Chances are, they didn't even look like opportunities at all. So now quite a few Dragons have retreated into a sulk. They greatly resent having their wings clipped.

Well, the good news is that 2021 will be different, Dragon. If you curb that fiery temper and resolve to adopt a mature attitude at all times, the Year of the Golden Ox will be the year when the fruits of success you earned in 2020 will finally arrive. Because even though you may not be aware of it yet, you managed to score quite a few hits last year. The benefits you should have enjoyed have been delayed a little, that's all.

This is because change had to happen – for everyone. It probably wasn't the type of change you had in mind, but there's a positive side for you in all the upheavals of the past 12 months, and this will become more and more obvious as 2021 unfolds.

Oddly enough, Ox years are often less than ideal for Dragons. The Ox and the Dragon are not naturally drawn to each other. Down to earth Ox is unimpressed by Dragon's showy charms – as Ox would see them – while the Dragon finds Ox a bit slow and dull.

Yet the Ox is always fair-minded and will respect genuine effort and quality work. So, as this year opens with many a Dragon yet to experience the rewards for past endeavors, the Ox will step in to help them materialize. It's only fair, after all.

What's more, the gentle metal energy that wafts in, in 2021, doesn't faze confident Dragon, (unlike the more cautious Rabbit), particularly as it breathes money into Dragon's bank account. Then there's the fact that, deep down, Dragon recognizes the Ox as a water creature while Dragons belong to the wood family and water is believed to be nurturing to wood. The Dragon knows that while bad behavior won't be tolerated, this relationship ensures Ox will always try to help, should genuine difficulties arise.

The result of all this is that Dragons that carry on with the plans begun, or reluctantly abandoned, last year – suitably updated of course – can expect to see them blossom into great achievements. Any kind of in-depth research into new ventures, new career ideas, or training schemes will prove rewarding, and finances should continue to improve. In fact, many employed Dragons can look forward to a pay rise or a promotion this year.

Intriguingly, whether you're a male or a female Dragon, your basic Dragon energy is regarded as strong, with a masculine quality. In 2021, however, the energy circulating has a subtle, feminine feel. This means that – this year – it is women who will bring you luck. Female friends, female bosses, and female colleagues are the people who will help you most. So seek out the women in your life, Dragon, and your fortunes will soar.

What it means to be a Dragon

To be honest, Dragon, it's not really fair. Your sign has so many advantages. When you're on good form, your personality is so dazzling the other signs need sunglasses.

The only mythical creature in the celestial cycle, in China the Dragon is associated with the Emperor and revered as a symbol of protection, power, and magnificence. No New Year celebration would be complete without the colourful Dragon, dancing through the streets, twisting and turning, and banishing evil spirits.

The Dragon is regarded as the most fortunate of signs and every couple hopes for a Dragon baby. A child born in a Dragon year is believed to bring good luck to the whole family and, to this day, the birth rate tends to rise about 5% in the Chinese community in Dragon years.

Dragons are usually strong, healthy, and blessed with enormous self-confidence and optimism. Even if they're not conventionally good-looking, they stand out in a crowd. They're charismatic with magnetic personalities, formidable energy, and people look up to them. Dragons are so accustomed to attention, they rarely question why this should be the case. It just seems like the natural way of the world.

These people think BIG. They're visionaries, bubbling with original new ideas, and their enthusiasm is so infectious, their optimism so strong, they easily inspire others. Without even trying, Dragons are born leaders and happily sweep their teams of followers into whatever new venture they've just dreamed up.

The only downside to this is that Dragons are easily bored. Trivial matters – such as details – irritate them, and they're keen to rush on to the next challenge before they've quite finished the first.

With a good second in command, who can attend to the picky minutiae, all could be well. If not, Dragon's schemes can go spectacularly wrong. Yet it hardly seems to matter. The Dragon ascribes to the theory that you have to fail your way to success. Setbacks are quickly forgotten as Dragon launches excitedly into the next adventure and quite often – given the Dragon's good luck – this works.

People born under this sign often receive success and wealth, yet they are not materialistic. They're generous and kind in an absent-minded way, and care far more about having a worthy goal than any rewards it might bring. And it is vital for the Dragon to have a goal. A Dragon without a goal is a sad, dispirited creature – restless and grumpy.

Even if it's not large, the Dragon home gives the impression of space and light. Dragons hate to feel confined in any way. They like to look out the window and see lots of sky and have clear, uncluttered surfaces around them, even if it's difficult for Dragons to keep them that way.

Yet the Dragon home could have a curiously un-lived-in feel. This is because the Dragon regards home as a lair – a comfortable base from which to plan the next project, rather than a place to spend a lot of time.

Dragons love to travel, but they don't really mind where they go as long as it's different and interesting. Yet, despite so much going for them, Dragons often feel misunderstood. Their impatience with trivia extends to the irritating need for tact and diplomacy at times. Dragon doesn't get this. If Dragon has something to say, they say it. Why waste time dressing it up in fancy words they think? But then people get upset, and Dragon is baffled. It's not always easy being a Dragon.

Best Jobs for Dragon

Actor

Environmental campaigner

Managing Director

Explorer

Barrister

Innovator

Perfect Partners

Cupid's arrow can strike anywhere at any time, of course, but once the novelty of new romance wears off, some relationships are easier to maintain than others. Here's a guide to the Dragon's compatibility with other signs.

Dragon with Dragon

When Dragon meets Dragon, onlookers tend to take a step back and hold their breath. These two are a combustible mix – they either love each other or loathe each other. They are so alike it could go either way. Both dazzling in their own orbits, they can't fail to notice the other's charms, but since they both need to be centre stage, things could get competitive. With give and take and understanding this match could work well, but it won't be easy.

Dragon with Snake

Surprisingly, this couple gets along beautifully. Snake's elegant appearance and quick but subtle mind intrigues Dragon, while Snake admires Dragon's success and endless energy. Snake has no need to battle for the limelight and is quite happy to sit back and support Dragon's schemes from the comfort of a stylish sofa. Which is all the encouragement Dragon needs.

Dragon with Horse

The athletic Horse is pretty good at keeping up with dashing Dragon. And Dragon appreciates a partner who enjoys getting out and about as much as Dragon does. Yet Horse might grow weary of Dragon's constant new projects and resent having to be involved. Horse likes to go off and do Horsey things at frequent intervals which Dragon tends to view as disloyal. This relationship could get fiery.

Dragon with Goat

Goat tends to baffle the busy Dragon. Dragon can see Goat is the creative type but can't understand why Goat doesn't appear to be working very hard when so much could be achieved. In fact, if they stayed together long enough, Dragon could help Goat make the most of many talents, but it's unlikely either of them can sustain enough interest for this to happen.

Dragon with Monkey

These two are likely to hit it off immediately. Each is attracted to the other's intelligence and lively presence, and Dragon's exuberance doesn't overwhelm hyperactive Monkey. What's more, though they both enjoy being surrounded by a crowd, Monkey only wants to make people laugh while Dragon hopes to inspire them to a cause. There is no conflict, so this couple can help each other to go far.

Dragon with Rooster

A Dragon and Rooster pairing will always attract attention. These two are both gorgeous beings and love to be surrounded by admirers. They will probably enjoy going out together and being seen as a couple, but in the long-term, they may not be able to provide the kind of support each secretly needs.

Entertaining for a while but probably not a lasting relationship.

Dragon with Dog

Not the easiest of combinations. Down-to-earth Dog can't see what all the fuss is about when it comes to Dragons. Unimpressed by glamour and irritated by what seems to Dog the gullibility of Dragon admirers, Dog can't be bothered to find out more. Dragon meanwhile is hurt by Dog's lack of interest. Great determination would be needed to make this work.

Dragon with Pig

While Dragon and Pig might seem to be opposites, the two of them can create a surprisingly contented relationship. Pig is quite happy for Dragon to fly around doing exciting things as long as Pig is not expected to do much more than admire profusely. Dragon appreciates Pig's uncritical support and makes allowances for Pig's lack of stamina. This couple could live in harmony.

Dragon with Rat

This couple is usually regarded as a very good match. They have much in common being action-loving, excitement-seeking personalities who hate to be bored. It takes a lot to dazzle Rat, but the Dragon's glamorous aura proves irresistible, while Dragon loves to be admired, so each enjoys being with the other. There could be the odd power struggle as these two are both strong characters but the magnetism is so powerful they usually kiss and make up.

Dragon with Ox

Chalk and cheese though this pair may appear to be, there's a certain fascination between them. Ox may not approve of Dragon's showy manner but recognises Dragon's good intentions, while Dragon admires Ox's strength of character and gift for completing tasks. If each could find a way to tolerate the other's wildly different lifestyles, they might be good for each other but, long-term, Dragon's hectic pace might wear down even the Ox's legendary stamina.

Dragon with Tiger

The two biggest personalities in the zodiac would seem bound to clash. After all, these larger than life characters share so many similarities there's a danger they'd compete. Yet a relationship between the Tiger and Dragon often works well. They understand each other's impulsive natures, but they're also different enough to supply the support the other needs. They'd make a formidable power couple.

Dragon with Rabbit

Dragon is such a larger than life character, Rabbit could feel overwhelmed at times. Also, the Dragon can be rather noisy and over-dramatic which would get on Rabbit's nerves. Yet they each admire the other's good points. If they could live next door to each other instead of under the same roof, a long-term relationship might work.

Dragon Love 2021 Style

No matter whether you're tall or short, dark or fair, the typical Dragon is a good-looking creature with tremendous presence. Dragons get noticed wherever they go – which is fine with Dragons, who are not typically known for their shy, retiring ways.

This year, love is in the air for many fire-breathers. Single Dragons only have to turn up at any gathering to attract admirers, and the softer, more romantic vibe of 2021 could lead to relationships turning serious, fast. Many Dragons could find themselves getting married this year or at least setting the date for a wedding.

Strangely enough, though they're flamboyant, bold, and full of confidence, Dragons don't really like being on their own. They can have their pick of new relationships, but – infuriatingly for other signs that are not so lucky – they don't seem to appreciate their good fortune in this respect nearly enough. The truth is, typical Dragons are much more comfortable knowing there's a loving partner waiting for them at home – even if they don't actually feel the need to spend too much time in that home. They are perfectly content to settle down. This year, with the family-oriented Ox at the helm, they'll get plenty of encouragement.

Attached Dragons can look forward to a happy year with their beloved. You'll get the chance to deepen your relationship in 2021, Dragon, as long as you don't succumb to temptation along the way. That ring on your finger won't deter single signs from trying their luck.

Secrets of Success in 2021

Basically, you just need to keep on doing what you've been doing Dragon. You were on the right track last year, even if your plans were interrupted and you didn't realize it. If an idea for a new direction came to you, chances are you should pursue it now.

The way to shoot yourself in the foot, Dragon, is to allow your natural enthusiasm and confidence to come across as ego, or bossiness. The Ox can't stand arrogance, so act modestly at all times, and fortune will smile on you. Then there's your tendency to start a project full of excitement only to get bored before it's finished and move on.

This habit needs to be curbed in 2021, Dragon. The Ox does not appreciate a grasshopper approach. Ox sticks to the task in hand, until it's complete, and you should do the same.

If you can avoid these pitfalls, you'll do brilliantly this year, Dragon. And keep in mind that working with women – as colleagues, partners or employers – will be especially fortunate for you in 2021.

The Dragon Year at a Glance

January – Things are getting better and better, Dragon. Cash is rolling in; you're feeling optimistic.

February – Your career is thriving, and new opportunities are on the way, Dragon. Don't overdo it, though, or you'll be susceptible to colds and flu.

March – A stubborn character in your orbit could prove annoying. You'd be justified if you got irritated… but keep cool. They'll move on if you ignore their antics.

April – Tricky vibes are swirling in your vicinity. Don't allow overconfidence to cause you to take your eye off the ball. Mistakes could cost you.

May – Spring is tempting you out to play. That's fine. Everything's going well – you can afford to take a break.

June – You're tempted to splurge on some luxury item. Check your finances carefully. Only go ahead if you're absolutely sure you can afford it.

July – Suddenly, you're surrounded by friends. Social life is going well, and offers of help are there if you need them.

August – A stroke of luck brings a big smile to your face. This would be the perfect time to throw a party for everyone who's contributed.

September – Deceptive stars surround you. An envious person may be trying to cheat you out of something that's rightfully yours. Keep your eyes open and be on guard.

October – Phew, you seem to have side-stepped last month's problems. Honest faces now remain close. You can afford to relax.

November – A project you've been working on for quite a while reaches fruition. Great success looks likely.

December – Celebrations are in order. You deserve congratulations – just don't get carried away. Stay modest!

Lucky colors for 2021: Silver, Blue, Yellow, White

Lucky numbers for 2021: 6, 7, 9

CHAPTER 6: THE SNAKE

Snake Years

10 February 1929 – 29 January 1930

27 January 1941 – 14 February 1942

14 February 1953 – 2 February 1954

2 February 1965 – 20 January 1966

18 February 1977 – 6 February 1978

6 February 1989 – 26 January 1990

24 January 2001 – 11 February 2002

10 February 2013 – 30 January 2014

29 January 2025 – 16 February 2026

Natural Element: Fire

Will 2021 be a Golden Year for the Snake?

It's been a long time coming, Snake, but – at last – some awesome news. It looks like 2021 will be a wonderful year for the sensuous, sophisticated serpent.

Most of the signs had a strange time in 2020 but, in an odd way, the ups and downs of those tumultuous 12 months weren't too unsettling for the typical Snake, as long as you were fortunate enough to avoid health issues.

This is down to the Snake's unique abilities. Snakes have an extraordinary habit of shrugging off their skin every now and then and gliding away, all glistening and glossy and rejuvenated, to begin again on a new adventure. What's more, while this process is taking place, Snakes are perfectly content to wait – resting and conserving their energy – until the amazing transformation is complete.

Snakes understand that you can't rush these things. Everything happens at its own proper pace. Nothing is gained by impatience. So the conditions last year were actually quite tolerable for the typical Snake. By a fortunate coincidence, the periodic skin-shedding for many Snakes was scheduled to take place during last year's Year of the Rat, in preparation for the whole new life to come in the dawning era.

Enforced hours at home during the lockdown wouldn't have bothered most Snakes too much. In fact, a period of blissful idleness while the process was going on would have suited them very well. And if the sun happened to be shining, and Snake could find a comfy place to bask, so much the better.

So, the good news is that with 2020 out of the way, the typical Snake is now back on form and ready to emerge into 2021 with spanking fresh bodywork, renewed energy, and an eagerness to get started. What's more, the Golden Ox is on hand and only too ready to help you.

Surprisingly, the Ox and the Snake have always got along very well. Despite the fact they appear to be completely different creatures, they have a lot in common. Neither feels the need to impose themselves on others or court attention.

Neither likes to be hurried or forced to rush around. Yet, both will approach any task they agree to undertake with seriousness and a certain amount of perfectionism.

The Ox has a lot of respect for the Snake, and for this reason, anything you do this year, Snake, will proceed more smoothly than could normally be expected. You and the Ox are both artistic types, so Snakes involved in creative businesses will be especially blessed. Should you work with your hands, Snake, wonderful masterpieces will fly from your fingers as if by magic.

Quite a few Snake interests probably had to be put on hold last year, but this will turn out to be a fortunate delay. To be honest, Snake, you weren't really ready at the time, even though you thought you were. Whether it was changing your job, starting a business, or moving home – all excellent ideas in themselves – they required more inner preparation than you realized.

This year, the Ox will encourage you to move forward on your pet projects again, but to proceed slowly and carefully. Quite a few Snakes will be considering property in some way; buying a new place, moving home, or maybe planning some kind of investment. You will be dazzled by quite a few tempting prospects, Snake, but may decide 'not to decide' just yet.

Job offers may arrive out of the blue, plus mouth-watering opportunities to increase your income. Yet you may find that despite these good omens, you keep coming across critical or unenthusiastic types who try to rain on your parade. This is likely to be because Snake belongs to the Fire family of zodiac creatures while the Ox, though friendly, is at heart a water animal – and Fire and Water are not normally a good mix.

Deep down, Snake can never forget that water could put out serpent fire, while Ox is aware that too much fire could overwhelm the Ox water. The result is a certain wariness beneath the surface which could manifest in day to day life as awkward, defensive individuals frequently crossing your path, causing irritation.

Yet these downbeat types won't succeed in spoiling your year, Snake. You can rise above their taunts. They're probably jealous anyway. The metal element of the year is bringing you money. Typical Snakes enjoyed an improving bank balance last year, and this trend will continue – which could prove galling for some less fortunate signs.

New projects could suddenly take flight, and female friends and colleagues could prove especially lucky right now. The Ox is not a great socializer but appreciates a close, dedicated team, so Snakes that surround themselves with a trusted inner circle will zoom ahead at twice the pace.

Family ties are set to get stronger and more meaningful this year, and though the Ox is not particularly interested in travel, homely trips with family and old friends are likely to be enjoyable and rewarding.

What it Means to Be a Snake

Imagine for a moment, a creature that was incredibly beautiful, wise, intelligent, graceful, sophisticated and respected. A creature always unhurried, yet attaining its goals, apparently without effort.

What would you call this amazing beast? Well if you were Chinese, you'd probably call it a Snake. That's right – a Snake.

Here, in the West, Snakes are almost as unwelcome as Rats and have been ever since Eve was persuaded to eat that apple in the Garden of Eden by a wily serpent. Most of us wouldn't have a good word to say for Snakes. Yet, in the East, it's a different story. There, all manner of positive qualities are discerned in the Snake, and the zodiac Snake is a good sign to be born under.

What's more, if we can forget all preconceived notions and look afresh at the much-maligned serpent, we have to admit there's something quite remarkable – almost magical – about the Snake.

For a start, Snakes don't have eyelids, which makes their stare particularly disconcerting. Astonishingly, they can shed their entire skins without ill effect, and slide away with a brand new, rejuvenated, wrinkle-free body – a feat many a human would envy.

Then there's the way they slither along without the need for legs – a bit repellent to a lot of people, but it can't be denied there's something uncanny about it. It's a surprisingly efficient means of locomotion too, and at times Snakes can move with astonishing speed. Quite a few of them can do this in water as well as on land, which makes them remarkably adaptable.

Snakes are in no way cuddly, but it seems even in the West we've retained a faint memory of a time when we recognized wisdom in the serpent. The Rod of Asclepius – the familiar symbol of a snake twisted around a pole – is still a widely used and recognised medical sign, seen outside pharmacies and doctors' surgeries, even if we don't know that Asclepius was the Greek God associated with healing. And in Greece, in the dim and distant past, snakes were sacred and believed to aid the sick.

The Chinese zodiac Snake is regarded as possibly the most beautiful of all the creatures, and people born under this sign somehow manage to present themselves in such an artful way, they give the illusion of beauty, even if not naturally endowed.

The Snake is physically graceful too. Each movement flowing into the next with effortless, elegant economy. Even when they're in a hurry, Snakes appear calm and unrushed, and should they arrive late for an appointment they're so charming and plausible with their excuses they're always forgiven.

This is a sign of great intelligence and subtlety. Snakes are never pushy, yet can usually slide into the heart of any situation they choose. Their clever conversation and easy charm makes them popular at any gathering. Yet, the Snake is picky. Snakes prefer to conserve their energy and don't waste it on activities and people of no interest to them. They are self-contained, quite happy with their own company if necessary, and seldom bored.

At work, Snakes are quietly ambitious, but in line with their policy of conserving energy wherever possible, they will aim for the quickest, easiest route to their goals. Just as the mythical Snake crossed the celestial river wrapped around the hoof of the Horse, the Snake is quite content to link their fortunes to those of a rising star so that Snake is carried to the top in their wake. Ever practical, the Snake has no need for an ego massage – the end result is what matters.

Other signs often mistake Snake's economy of action for laziness, but this is short-sighted. In fact, the Snake is so efficient and so clever that tasks are completed with great speed, leaving Snake with plenty of time to relax afterwards. What's more, in the same way that a Snake can shed its skin, people born under this sign are quite capable of suddenly walking out of a situation or way of life that no longer suits them, and reinventing themselves elsewhere without regret.

They tend to do this without warning, leaving their previous companions stunned. Only afterwards do people learn that the Snake has been inert and silently brooding for months. But it's no good imploring Snake to return. Snake's actions are swift and irrevocable.

The Snake home is a lovely place. Snakes have perfect taste. They like art, design, good lighting, and comfort. They're excellent hosts. They may not often entertain, unless they can delegate the chores, but when they do, they make it a stylish occasion to remember.

Snakes are known for their love of basking in the sun, and zodiac Snakes are no exception. Trips involving long hikes uphill in the pouring rain will not impress the Snake, but a smart sun-lounger by an infinity pool in a tropical paradise... well, that would be Snake's idea of heaven.

Best Jobs for Snake

Diplomat

Psychologist

Radiologist

Therapist

Nail technician

Designer

Tarot card reader

Perfect Partners

Cupid's arrow can strike anywhere at any time, of course, but once the novelty of new romance wears off, some relationships are easier to maintain than others. Here's a guide to the Snake's compatibility with other signs.

Snake with Snake

This fine looking couple turn heads wherever they go. Beautiful and perfectly dressed these two look like the perfect match. They never stop talking and enjoy the same interests so this could be a successful relationship. Long-term, however, there could be friction. They're both experts at getting what they want using the same sophisticated techniques, so they can see through each other.

Snake with Horse

At some level, perhaps, Horse remembers how Snake beat him in the calendar race, so despite an initial attraction, these two could be wary of each other. Snake is impressed by Horse's energy and athleticism while Horse admires Snake's elegance and charm. Yet they don't really have much in common. Deep thinking Snake could find Horse rather shallow and Horse may see Snake as frustratingly enigmatic.

Snake with Goat

Snake and Goat could enjoy many happy hours touring art galleries and exhibitions together. Neither of them craves excitement and harsh, adrenaline-boosting activities, and both appreciate creative artistic personalities. There's no pressure to compete with each other so these two would sail along quite contentedly. Not a passionate alliance but they could be happy.

Snake with Monkey

These two clever creatures ought to admire each other if only for their fine minds and, at first, it's possible they might. But unless they're really determined to make it work, it won't be long before active Monkey finds Snake's energy-saving ways irritating, while Snake loses patience with Monkey's endless jokes.

Snake with Rooster

Surprisingly, Snake and Rooster work well together. Both gorgeous in different ways, they complement each other without competing. Snake's keen eyes can see beneath Rooster's proud facade to the sensitive, unsure person inside, while Rooster appreciates Snake's unobtrusive strength and wise words of encouragement at just the right moment. These two could be inseparable.

Snake with Dog

Some snakes seem to have an almost hypnotic power and, for some reason, Dog is particularly susceptible to these skills. We've heard of snake-charmers, but snakes can be dog-charmers and, without even trying, Snakes can find themselves the recipients of Dog devotion. Since the Dog is strong, loyal, and can be fun, Snake is not averse to this but might, in the end, find it boring.

Snake with Pig

Pig and Snake don't have a lot to say to each other. Snake can't be bothered with Pig's endless shopping, and Pig is hurt by Snake's snobbish attitude. They both enjoy the good things in life so a luxury fling could briefly be fun – a shared spa break might be a good idea – but in the long-term, this relationship is probably not worth pursuing.

Snake with Rat

The Snake shares Rat's good taste and being elegant, sophisticated, and smart will delight Rat at first sight. These two get on very well on an intellectual level but perhaps are better as good friends rather than long-term partners. The Snake's love of basking in the sun for hours strikes Rat as lazy and dull, while Rat's need to rush around doing deals and meeting people seems pointless and wearying to Snake.

Snake with Ox

Like Ox, the Snake is quietly ambitious and not given to racing around unless it's absolutely necessary. Ox, on the other hand, respects Snake's clever brain and understated elegance. These two could quickly discover how beneficial an alliance between them would be. They're both happy to give the other space when required but also step in with support when needed. This could be a very successful match.

Snake with Tiger

Not the best of romances. These two are so fundamentally different that any initial attraction is unlikely to last. Snake likes to bask and soak up the sun while Tiger wants to explore and discover. Tiger takes in the big picture at a glance and is off to the next challenge while Snake likes to pause, delve beneath the surface, and consider matters. It wouldn't take long before these two annoy each other.

Snake with Rabbit

This subtle pair could make a good combination. They both understand the value of working behind the scenes and neither has any desire to wear themselves out on endless adventures. They share a love of art, fine things, and quiet pleasures and they both enjoy an orderly home. These two could settle down very happily together.

Snake with Dragon

Surprisingly, this couple gets along beautifully. Snake's elegant appearance and quick but subtle mind intrigues Dragon, while Snake admires Dragon's success and endless energy. Snake has no need to battle for the limelight and is quite happy to sit back and support Dragon's schemes from the comfort of a stylish sofa. Which is all the encouragement Dragon needs.

Snake Love 2021 Style

The sexy, sensuous Snake is never short of admirers despite a tendency to sit back and let interested parties make all the running. This year is no exception. Both single and attached Snakes exercise an effortless, magnetic appeal which is even stronger in 2021 as Snake is bathed in the golden glow of the approving Ox.

Yet the typical Snake is picky. Snake is not interested in accepting invitations for the sake of them, or which massage the serpent ego. Most prospective partners will find themselves staring in bewilderment at Snakes rapidly receding back after a few moments of delightful conversation. What went wrong, they ask themselves. The chances are, they'll never know.

The year of the Ox will bring endless opportunities for romance, Snake, and single Snakes in the mood for a dalliance will take full advantage. Attached Snakes may do the same.

Yet so soon after your recent relaunch, it's quite likely you're not ready for anything resembling settling down yet. You've hardly got your restructured life up and running. Who knows where it may lead and who you may like to share it with?

Annoyingly the loyal, traditionally-minded Ox is keen to encourage pairing up in a faithful manner this year, so it's likely that – once again – many Snakes will be fending off more than their fair share of lovelorn offers. But this is a finely honed skill by now, so there won't be much soul-searching involved for the typical serpent.

And, if by chance, some special person did manage to overcome the Snake defenses, this could actually turn out to be a very good year to make it permanent. But you're in no hurry, Snake.

Secrets of Success in 2021

You've got everything to play for this year, Snake, and this is certainly the time to make a big effort. Since you work best behind the scenes, few people even notice the serpent skills being put into action, but the Ox is sympathetic to your mode of operations.

Your main problem will be your tendency to silent impatience. In 2021, you'll be surrounded by jobsworths who insist on dotting every i and crossing every t before making a move. Their attitude could set you hissing with fury. Yet since the Snake is outwardly the very picture of indolence, few realize you're capable of lightning speed when the occasion demands.

Quite often this year, it will seem as if the occasion is highly demanding and you're more than willing to react swiftly, yet those annoying jobsworths keep dragging you back. Try not to lose your temper, Snake, or you could risk ruining a promising opportunity. Keep cool and smile sweetly. The truth is you've got plenty of time. The Ox prefers a ponderous pace. You can afford to sit back and wait for the others to catch up. Do it with good grace and success is yours.

The Snake Year at a Glance

January – It's the New Year, and you're feeling good, Snake. You're looking good, too. Keep an eye out for jealous glances coming your way.

February – Is it the sales, or are you just keen to treat yourself? Money is burning through your hands this month. Stick to a budget if you can.

March – The days grow longer, and you're in the mood for getting out. Colleagues are argumentative though. Rise above their negativity.

April – Work is going well. Someone in authority is impressed with your efforts.

May – Keep doing what you're doing, Snake. Great opportunities abound in your career.

June – An old flame reappears. They're looking for romance but maybe something more too. Think carefully before you agree to help.

July – Whether it's that old flame or someone else, be careful with your cash this month. Try not to lend or be talked into reckless purchases.

August – Summer is smiling, and you may get news of a pay rise or windfall of some kind. Celebrate by taking a relaxing holiday.

September – An offer arrives out of the blue. Decisions, decisions. Think carefully before you make up your mind.

October – Watch out, Snake, you could be the subject of a disagreement. Two lovers or maybe just two friends are arguing over you. Keep a low profile.

November – Only November, but you're starting to feel Christmassy. Things are going well, and you're looking forward to fun.

December – Big celebrations are in order. There's money in the bank so you can afford to splurge on some fabulous presents.

Lucky colors for 2021: Orange, Red, Purple

Lucky numbers 2021: 9, 4

CHAPTER 7: THE HORSE

Horse Years

30 January 1930 – 16 February 1931

15 February 1942 – 4 February 1943

3 February 1954 – 23 January 1955

21 January 1966 – 8 February 1967

7 February 1978 – 27 January 1979

27 January 1990 – 14 February 1991

12 February 2002 – 31 January 2003

31 January 2014 – 18 February 2015

17 February 2026 – 5 February 2027

Natural Element: Fire

Will 2021 be a Golden Year for the Horse?

The magnificent zodiac Horse should be trotting into 2021 with head held high, tail swishing, and feeling good. That's because one of the best things you've got going for you in the Year of the Golden Ox, Horse, is robust health and vitality – which must be wonderful news.

Last year was a tricky one for all the signs, but possibly for the freedom-loving Horse it was especially frustrating. Even if the Horse is not planning to go anywhere, the typical equine has to feel – at all times – as if they could, should the idea suddenly appeal. Being forced to stay indoors and at home is likely to bring on claustrophobia.

Even without Covid-19, 2020 was destined to have quite a few awkward moments for many Horses. This is because the Rat, which ruled the year, and the Horse don't really understand each other, so it would have taken a lot of effort on Horses' part to keep things running smoothly. Add a virus and compulsory quarantine to the mix, and it would have been near impossible for most Horses to remain on an even keel for long. So if you got a bit moody and temperamental at times, Horse, nobody could blame you.

Fortunately, 2021 is set to be different. Not perfect, Horse, because it has to be said that you and the Golden Ox are not best buddies either. While the Ox can admire your wonderful style and speed, the admiration is a bit grudging. There could even be a little jealousy involved. On the face of it, you've got a lot in common – you're both big, strong, muscular creatures, very useful to have around a farm. Yet, when it comes to speed and good looks – well, you leave the poor old Ox standing, don't you? Who could blame Ox for feeling resentful?

So, this year, you've got to earn your good fortune, Horse. But that's entirely possible because the other great thing about the Ox is its sense of justice. Impartial Ox will not let any lingering negative feelings deprive you of credit where credit is due.

For this reason, employed Horses can expect to do well at work if they put in the hours. Freelance Horses can expect unusual opportunities to roll over the horizon. Teamwork is particularly favored this year, so for those Horses that can round up colleagues and pool talents, the sky really could be the limit, whether you're employed, freelance, or building your own business.

One of the difficulties last year, was the fact that – deep down – the Rat is believed to be a water creature while Horse belongs to the fire family. As we know, fire and water don't mix. In fact, fire is distinctly nervous around water for obvious reasons. So out in the world, in practical terms, this uneasiness between you could manifest as a sense of anxiety, regularly nagging away at the back of your mind for no obvious reason, or the annoying experience of endlessly encountering argumentative types just longing to be uncooperative.

Unfortunately, this year's Golden Ox – like the Rat – is also a water animal, so the same tricky fire and water issues are likely to arise. The much better news, though, is that Ox's energy is different – far softer and milder than Rat's – so although similar underlying challenges could recur, they won't bother you nearly so much. In fact, some Horses will scarcely notice them at all.

This means that Horse can look forward to a more relaxed year in 2021. Anxious feelings should be easier to calm, and where – last year – there were temper tantrums in your orbit, now you're likely to encounter mere misunderstandings. With patience and your usual charm, Horse, you should be able to sort things out agreeably.

The metal element of 2021 will direct a boost of cash very pleasingly your way but resist the temptation to spend, spend, spend. The flow is likely to be sporadic, and those misunderstandings could cause hold-ups. Wise Horses will stash away their windfalls. By the end of the year, you'll be amazed at your increased wealth.

You'll certainly be busy this year, Horse, and the metal element could normally make you feel a bit overwhelmed and tired. Yet, since you're blessed with good health in 2021, you'll be able to do twice as much as usual and still have energy to spare. Chances are, you'd love to make the most of that get-up-and-go by taking off on an exotic break. But this is probably not the best plan right now. Ox isn't a big traveler, so long-distance jaunts could come fraught with difficulties. A number of intriguing staycations will prove fortunate and could turn out to be much more fun than you imagined; once you discover a special place, you'll be drawn back over and over again.

Even if you never thought of yourself as the sporty type, this year, Horse, you could get in touch with your inner athlete. In fact, you could discover a talent you had no idea you possessed. Whether you hit the gym, buy a bike, or take up wind-surfing, it looks like you'll amaze yourself and all your friends with your unexpected skill. This could be a source of pleasure for years to come.

What it means to be a Horse

Sleek and graceful, as well as strong and swift, the Horse has always been an object of admiration and often longing. Young girls dream of having their own pony while many adults, on acquiring a pile of cash, often treat themselves to a racehorse or at least a share in one.

In China, the Horse is believed to be a symbol of freedom, and you've only got to see a picture of the famous white horses of the Camargue, exuberantly splashing through the marshes, to understand why.

People born in the year of the Horse exude a similar magnificence. They tend to be strong and athletic with broad shoulders and fine heads of thick hair. Where would the Horse be without its mane? Most Horses excel at sports, especially when young. They can run fast if they choose, but they will happily try any game until they find the one that suits them best.

Horses, being herd animals, are gregarious types and don't like to spend too long alone. They enjoying hanging out with a crowd, chatting and swapping gossip, and Horses of both sexes can lap up any amount of grooming. They love having their hair brushed and fussed over, their nails manicured; a facial or relaxing massage is usually welcome.

Yet, Horses are more complex than they first appear. The affable, easy-going charmer, delighting everyone at a party, can suddenly take offence at a casual remark or storm off in a huff over some tiny hitch almost unnoticeable to anyone else, leaving companions baffled. They tend to stay baffled too, because it's difficult to get a handle on what upsets the Horse since what annoys them one week may leave them completely unruffled the next.

The trouble is, although they look tough, Horses are, in fact, very sensitive. Inside, they're still half-wild. Their senses are incredibly sharp, and although they don't realize it, deep down they're constantly scanning the horizon and sniffing the air for the first signs of danger. As a result, Horses live on their nerves. They tend to over-react when things don't go completely to plan, and have to work hard to control a sense of panic. Ideally, Horses would like to bolt away when the going gets rough but as this is not usually possible, they get moody and difficult instead.

Provide calm, congenial conditions for a Horse, however, and you couldn't wish for a friendlier companion. The Horse is lively, enthusiastic, versatile, and fun.

At work, the Horse wants to do well but can't stand being fenced in or forced to perform repetitive, routine tasks. Also, although they're good in a team, Horses have a need for privacy and independence so they may change jobs frequently until they find the right role. Yet, when they're happy, Horses will shine.

At home, Horse is probably planning the next trip. Horses like to be comfortable but they're not the most domesticated of the signs. They love being in the open air and don't see the point of spending too much time wallowing on a sofa or polishing dusty ornaments. They may well spend more time in the garden than indoors. On holiday, Horse loves to head for wide-open spaces – a vast beach, a craggy hillside or a mountain meadow; Horse would be thrilled to explore them all.

Best Jobs for Horse

Sports commentator

Hairdresser

Beautician

Events manager

Horse Trainer

PE Teacher

Dancer

Perfect Partners

Cupid's arrow can strike anywhere at any time, of course, but once the novelty of new romance wears off, some relationships are easier to maintain than others. Here's a guide to the Horse's compatibility with other signs.

Horse with Horse

No doubt about it, these two make a magnificent couple, and any foals in the family would be spectacular. They certainly understand each other, particularly their shared need for both company and alone time so, in general, they get on well. The only tricky part could come if they both grew anxious over the same issue at the same time. Neither would find it easy to calm the other.

Horse with Goat

Goat and Horse just click! These two love kicking up their heels and trotting off into the green. Goat doesn't need to go far or do anything strenuous but is always up for a break in routine, while Horse doesn't do routine at all so is constantly on the lookout for a partner ready to escape. This couple rarely considers the consequences but, mostly, they don't need to.

Horse with Monkey

Uh oh – best not attempted unless it's love at first sight. Monkey and Horse have wildly different outlooks and can't seem to see eye to eye on anything. They're both lively but in different ways that don't complement each other. Monkey will consider Horse's moods illogical and pointless while Horse is irritated that Monkey makes no attempt to understand how Horse feels. Very hard work.

Horse with Rooster

The eye-catching Rooster intrigues Horse while Rooster appreciates Horse's strength and agility. They can enjoy many stimulating dates together. Yet, in the long-run, this couple may not be able to provide the stability the other needs. They're both sensitive types but in different ways. After a while, the relationship could run out of steam.

Horse with Dog

Both good friends of man, these two can make a formidable team. Dog understands the occasional need for solitude while admiring Horse's strength and agility. Horse, meanwhile, senses Dog's loyalty and down to earth nature. Both lovers of the great outdoors and physical activity, they'll never be short of adventures to share. A promising long-term relationship.

Horse with Pig

Pig and Horse are good companions. Horse is soothed by easy-going Pig and Pig is proud to be seen with such an alluring creature as Horse. They don't have a lot of interests in common, but they don't antagonize each other either. They can jog along amicably for quite a while, but long-term they may find they each want more than the other can provide.

Horse with Rat

Rat and Horse both fizz with energy, and they love action and looking good, yet this is not seen as an ideal partnership. Nothing's impossible of course, but these two will have to work hard to find harmony. The Rat will admire Horse's enthusiasm and cheerful approach but become impatient to discover Horse can also be fiery and emotional. Horse, on the other hand, can find Rat's risk-taking behavior extremely worrying.

Horse with Ox

Long ago on many Western farms, Ox was replaced by the Horse, and it may be that Ox has never forgotten and never forgiven. At any rate, these two, despite both being big, strong animals are not usually friends. Horse is too flighty and frivolous to interest Ox for long, while Ox's methodical, careful ways will irritate the Horse. Best not to go there.

Horse with Tiger

This athletic pair gets on pretty well. They both like physical pursuits, testing their strength out of doors or just enjoying the feel of the wind in their hair and the ground under their feet. True, Horse may not quite understand Tiger's plans for world domination, but it doesn't really matter. Horse is happy to be loyal to such a charismatic partner. As they're both moody, there could be rows but making up is exciting.

Horse with Rabbit

This could be tricky. It's fairly unlikely that Horse and Rabbit would ever end up on a date, but if they did and there was a strong attraction, it could lead to a love/hate relationship. Rabbit's neat and tidy ways would enrage Horse and Horse's unpredictable moods and over-the-top reactions would annoy Rabbit. Soon, Horse is likely to bolt for the hills or Rabbit retreat to its burrow.

Horse with Dragon

The athletic Horse is pretty good at keeping up with dashing Dragon. And Dragon appreciates a partner who enjoys getting out and about as much as Dragon does. Yet Horse might grow weary of Dragon's constant new projects and resent having to be involved. Horse likes to go off and do Horsey things at frequent intervals which Dragon tends to view as disloyal. This relationship could get fiery.

Horse with Snake

At some level, perhaps Horse remembers how Snake beat him in the calendar race, so despite an initial attraction, these two could be wary of each other. Snake is impressed by Horse's energy and athleticism while Horse admires Snake's elegance and charm. Yet they don't really have much in common. Deep thinking Snake could find Horse rather shallow, and Horse may see Snake as frustratingly enigmatic.

Horse Love 2021 Style

Right from day one, you'll be looking good, Horse, even if you don't deserve it after a long night's partying to welcome in the New Year. This is because the good health bestowed on you in 2021 will make your eyes sparkle, your hair shine, and your skin appear radiant. Even if you don't notice it yourself, others will.

All of which, of course, will render you even more attractive than usual. This is excellent news, naturally, but attached Horses need to take care. Those misunderstandings that are likely to arise out of nowhere this year could find themselves magnetically drawn to your love life. Partners are particularly prone to getting the wrong idea in 2021. Spend too long chatting to a new acquaintance, appear to be enjoying attention a little too much, or even checking your phone a little too frequently, and there could be trouble.

If you want the relationship to last, curb your independent streak, put on a modest smile, and do your best to make a fuss of your partner at every opportunity.

Single Horses, of course, can do as they please and bask in the compliments and invitations that will inevitably come along. Group activities and parties are particularly lucky for you right now, and true love may even appear. Yet don't expect a promising new relationship to run smoothly. They may be your soul mate, but due to the prickly nature of the energy this year, the two of you will need to make a big effort at times not to misunderstand each other. On the other hand, if you're still happily entwined by the end of the year, there could be wedding bells in 2022.

Secret of Success in 2021

You've got a lot of potential this year, Horse, but to make it work for you, you'll need to rein in some of your most Horsey traits. For a start, Ox demands patience. Which you'll have to admit isn't your strongest gift. When a task gets tricky, or throws up unexpected problems, the typical Horse tends to get irritated and inclined to abandon the whole thing. It's even been known for some Horses to throw a tantrum in such circumstances.

It might make you feel better at the time, Horse, but you won't profit in the long run. The Ox deplores this type of behavior and will make sure you learn the error of your ways. If you can develop stamina and stick with the project until it's complete, the rewards when you've finished the job will amaze you.

Then there's your need for independence. Despite being a herd animal, the typical Horse likes regular 'alone' time. This year, however, success is achieved more readily by working in a team. Find a way of balancing your 'me' time and individuality with the demands of fitting in with a group and being patient with everyone, and you just can't fail. In fact, you'll develop skills that will keep you winning for the rest of the decade.

The Horse Year at a Glance

January – Already you can feel your energy rising and confidence increasing. Organize your diary and streamline your activities – things will get busy.

February – Time to use the same approach on your social life. You're going to be in demand, so plan your time wisely.

March – Cash is looking for you, Horse. A pay rise, tax rebate, or some sort of windfall is on the way.

April – Someone in your orbit could do with a helping hand. Could be a colleague at work or a family member. Stay alert and be ready to step in.

May – Things are going well at work. Keep focused. Don't let outside distractions drag you off course.

June – You're popular with friends and colleagues. Summer fun is calling. Don't forget your responsibilities at work.

July – Maybe there's a heatwave but whatever the cause, fractious types surround you. Refuse to take sides and don't get involved in other people's disputes.

August – Time to relax and take a break. An unusual holiday will bring good fortune.

September – Another cash boost is on the way. Don't go crazy, Horse. A little treat perhaps and stash the rest?

October – You've hit your stride now. Clever Horses have found a beneficial way of working. Keep on doing what you're doing.

November – Unexpected bills could appear out of the blue. Good thing you saved some of that windfall. You did, didn't you Horse?

December – Party time is back again, and you're eager to play. Just watch out for those annoying types who always want to disagree. Don't rise to the bait, and all will be well.

Lucky colors for 2021: Orange, gold, pink

Lucky numbers for 2021: 7, 3, 9

CHAPTER 8: THE GOAT

Goat Years

17 February 1931 – 5 February 1932

5 February 1943 – 24 January 1944

24 January 1955 – 11 February 1956

9 February 1967 – 29 January 1968

28 January 1979 – 15 February 1980

15 February 1991 – 3 February 1992

1 February 2003 – 21 January 2004

19 February 2015 – 7 February 2016

6 February 2027 – 25 January 2028

Natural Element: Fire

Will 2021 be a Golden Year for the Goat?

Okay, Goat. You can come out from behind the sofa now. The hair-raising, roller-coaster ride that was 2020 has finally rattled away, and there's a very good chance 2021 will bring you much calmer times.

Perhaps more than any other sign, you need to feel safe and secure in order to make the most of your gentle, happy-go-lucky talents. When they see you cheerfully going about your business in that laid-back, bohemian way of yours, other signs assume the Goat must be the most tranquil and unruffled of creatures. They get the impression that nothing bothers you, but in truth, the typical Goat can only operate in that carefree way as long as peace and serenity surround them.

When unpleasant dramas strike, the Goat becomes quietly consumed with anxiety.

Few would suspect it, of course, because Goats are experts at displaying a brave face but deep down you're suffering, which is why the unexpected upheavals of the past year have been so difficult for many Goats.

The odd thing is that once you start sifting through the wreckage of your 2020 plans, you'll probably find some wonderful treasures. These could take the form of projects begun before the crisis hit that have somehow survived and look destined to bloom into success now the storm has abated, or they might turn out to be opportunities you scarcely noticed at the time but can now see for the promising possibilities they contain.

So, now we have a brand new year and every reason for Goats to be optimistic. It has to be admitted, though, that the Goat and ruler of the year – Ox – don't have much in common. They really don't 'get' each other and, for this reason, Ox years are not normally the easiest for the typical Goat to negotiate. Yet 2021 is different, simply by virtue of coming straight after the tsunami that was 2020.

The usual slight friction that can be expected for Goats (because of the lack of shared empathy with the Ox) will hardly register now, after all that has gone before, which leaves Goat free to enjoy the benefits that Ox years bring.

For a start, life will become quieter, less changeable, and more settled – the kind of conditions most Goats crave. As the weeks go on, the typical cloven hoofer will sense that inner tension start to unwind. And as you relax, so the natural Goat talents will resurface, and you can take advantage of the qualities you do actually share with the Ox.

Unlikely as it might seem, you are both highly creative personalities with strong, artistic gifts. Goats working in creative spheres will do exceptionally well this year. The Ox will pour good fortune on fine craftsmanship and devoted attention to detail. All of which come naturally to the Goat. And as 2021 is once again a 'metal' year, any occupation that involves metal in some way – from jewelry making, to sculpture, to embellishing fabrics with metallic trimmings, or creating useful items in a forge – is destined for success.

Despite this, it's probably not the best year to be thinking about changing jobs, unless absolutely essential. 2021 will reserve the finest rewards for those that build on existing foundations. Whatever was begun last year, or even earlier, is now ripe for extending, renovating, or relaunching. This goes for the Goat career, or the Goat home, or possibly both.

The other great thing about metal years is that they encourage the flow of cash – so you can expect a boost to your bank account, Goat. The trouble is, the cash does tend to 'flow'.

So it could flow out of your bank as quickly as it flows in, unless you're careful, Goat.

Typical Goats don't much care, of course, as long as they're enjoying the process. What's more, Goats have an uncanny knack of being able to take something quite mundane and transform it into a unique creation. This year, that talent will be greatly appreciated and admired. You could even make your name if you work hard at it Goat.

Though most Goats like to be on the move, they're not too fussed about particular destinations, which is just as well. The Ox is not a big traveler, so you'll probably find yourself opting for a number of breaks close to home. These could turn out to lead to some surprising opportunities. Even if you're not thinking of moving, Goat, you could well fall in love with somewhere you come across on your travels and end up living there.

What it Means to be a Goat

If people born under the sign of the Goat tend to look a little puzzled, uncertain even, who could blame them? It's not even definite their sign is the Goat. Some authorities call their sign the Sheep. Others – the more macho types – have it down as the Ram.

The confusion seems to stem from different translations of the original Chinese word.

But what's in a name? Whatever you call it, the qualities ascribed to the Goat/Sheep/Ram are the same. In China, the sign is regarded as symbolizing peace and harmony. What's more, it's the eighth sign of the zodiac and the number eight is believed to be a very lucky number, associated as it is with growth and prosperity.

So, all you confused Goats out there can relax in the knowledge you were born in a lucky year.

In truth, perhaps the gentle sheep – the living animal that is – does resemble the zodiac Goat more than the real-life goat. Flesh and blood goats tend to have a feisty, combative quality and a strongly stubborn streak. Those sharp, pointy horns and all that head-butting does tend to put people off.

Yet, people born in a Goat year are known as the sweetest and friendliest of all the signs. They possess no spikey quality at all. They are tolerant and kind, have no wish to be competitive, and want to see the best in everyone they meet. Though they may not realise it, this attitude often unconsciously brings out the best in others, so the Goat's expectations are usually fulfilled.

Goats seem to get on with almost everyone, even people that others can't abide.

What's more, Goats usually possess a wonderful artistic talent. Even those Goats who feel they can't paint, draw, or manage anything skilled, are nevertheless immensely creative with a fine eye for colour and design.

The Goat loves beautiful things and even sees beauty in objects and places that hold no appeal for others. They love to use their hands in their spare time, ideally making something practical yet decorative. Knitting, card-making, cake-decorating, gardening, or renovating old furniture, even DIY, will give them great pleasure.

Concepts such as time and also money, have little meaning for the Goat. When the Goat gets lost in inspiration, hours pass in seconds and Goat ends up late for anything else that might have been on the agenda.

Similarly, money is frustrating for the Goat. Goats are not materialistic; neither are they particularly ambitious in a worldly way. Objects other people regard as status symbols hold little Goat appeal so they can't see the point of putting in a lot of energy to acquire them. For this reason, Goats are not career-driven. All they really want to do is pursue their artistic project or latest interest. If this won't provide an income though, they'll do their best at whatever job turns up, in order to get back to their true vocation at weekends.

The perfect scenario for the Goat would be a big win on the lottery, so they never have to waste time on a conventional job again. Should this ever happen, they'd be advised to get someone else to look after the funds for them; Goats are not good at handling finances, and the windfall could slip through their fingers with distressing speed.

Goats are notoriously impractical with matters such as bills, household repairs, filling in forms, and meeting deadlines. They just can't seem to find the time to tackle such mundane items. Though they're intelligent people, they'll frequently claim not to understand such things. The truth is, of course, the ultra-creative Goat brain just can't be bothered.

One thing Goats do have in common with the flesh and blood animal is their stubborn streak. Despite that easy-going, sunny nature, zodiac Goats can astonish their friends by suddenly digging in their heels over what looks to others like a trivial matter of very little importance. Once Goat has adopted this position, it will not budge, no matter how unreasonable or how poor the outcome is likely to be.

The Goat home is an intriguing place. Striking and original, it's likely to be filled with mismatched treasures Goat has picked up along the way. Goats love car boot sales, junk shops, and galleries. They enjoy beach-combing and collecting branches and broken wood on country walks. They've even been known to 'rescue' items from rubbish skips. Somehow, Goat manages to weave together the most unpromising items to create a pleasing effect.

Best Jobs for Goat

Artist

Potter

Interior Designer

Personal shopper

Make-up artist

Photographer

Furniture Restorer

Perfect Partners

Cupid's arrow can strike anywhere at any time, of course, but once the novelty of new romance wears off, some relationships are easier to maintain than others. Here's a guide to the Goat's compatibility with other signs.

Goat with Goat

When things are going well, you won't find a happier couple than two Goats. They are perfectly in tune with each other's creative natures and understand when to do things together and when to step back and give the other space. And since they both share the same interests, their together times are always fun. Yet, when practical problems arise, neither can easily cope. With a helpful friend on speed-dial, this would work.

Goat with Monkey

Monkey and Goat are different but in a good way. Though they don't quite 'get' each other deep down, Goat admires Monkey's lively personality and magical ability to come up with solutions for everything, while curious Monkey enjoys Goat's knowledge of the arts and the unusual. Long-term, Goat might not present enough of a challenge for Monkey but, with effort, it's a promising match.

Goat with Rooster

Peaceful Goat is not one to make feathers fly, so these two are unlikely to fall out, but they're unlikely to find perfect compatibility either. Goat is unable to give Rooster the regular ego boosts that make Rooster thrive while Rooster is baffled by Goat's unpredictable devotion to impractical projects or people. Misunderstandings are likely.

Goat with Dog

This is another relationship that could be tricky. Loyal Dog would be quite willing to stand by Goat when practical problems loom but could end up irritated by Goat's inability to learn from previous mistakes and so keeps making them. Goat can't understand why Dog gets so bothered. With care, these two could learn to live together.

Goat with Pig

Happy-go-lucky Pig and laid-back Goat make a good pair. They hate to stir up trouble and always look for a peaceful solution to any challenge. Ideally, they'd avoid the challenge altogether. They could be very contented together as long as Pig's spending and Goat's inability to deal with finances doesn't get them into trouble.

Goat with Rat

The Rat is charmed by carefree Goat and fascinated by its artistic talent and happy knack of living in the present. Easy-going Goat tends to like everyone so is perfectly content to enjoy Rat's company. These two can get along fine, yet they don't really understand each other deep down. Long-term, the Rat may find Goat's lack of interest in the practical side of life irritating.

Goat with Ox

Though these two share artistic natures (even if in the case of the Ox, they're well hidden), deep down they don't 'get' one another. Ox may be beguiled at first by Goat's friendly, easy-going manner but then disappointed to discover Goat seems to find everyone equally delightful, even those who are plainly unworthy. Goat, on the other hand, can't understand why Ox won't lighten up more. This relationship would require a lot of effort and compromise.

Goat with Tiger

Tiger and Goat don't have a lot in common. While their aims and temperaments are quite different, they are both sociable creatures and Goat wouldn't mind Tiger attracting all the attention when they're out together. Tiger, in return, would appreciate Goat's lack of jealousy and generosity of spirit. Yet, long-term, they're likely to drift apart as they follow their different interests.

Goat with Dragon

Goat tends to baffle the busy Dragon. Dragon can see Goat is the creative type but can't understand why Goat doesn't appear to be working very hard when so much could be achieved. In fact, if they stayed together long enough, Dragon could help Goat make the most of many talents but it's unlikely either of them can sustain enough interest for this to happen.

Goat with Snake

Snake and Goat could enjoy many happy hours touring art galleries and exhibitions together. Neither of them craves excitement and harsh, adrenaline-boosting activities and both appreciate creative, artistic personalities. There's no pressure to compete with each other so these two would sail along quite contentedly. Not a passionate alliance but they could be happy.

Goat with Horse

Goat and Horse just click! These two love kicking up their heels and trotting off into the green. Goat doesn't need to go far or do anything strenuous but is always up for a break in routine, while Horse doesn't do routine at all so is constantly on the lookout for a partner ready to escape. This couple rarely considers the consequences, but mostly, they don't need to.

Goat Love 2021 Style

Single Goats could be in for a surprise this year. Some occasion is likely to come along when they've not dressed up, or even bothered to brush their hair, and suddenly they bump into a past love or maybe just a past crush. Of course, the typical Goat looks original and stylish without even trying so they'll look good anyway, though chances are they'll be mortified. But if this is you, Goat, there's a strong possibility you'll end up seeing this person again. And again.

What will come of it? It all depends on why it went wrong first time around, or why they failed to notice you back then and how much things have now changed. But you'll have great fun seeing where this new romance leads.

Attached Goats may find partners a little argumentative this year. The typical Goat always tries to avoid disagreements if at all possible, so chances are you're an expert at defusing tricky situations. Make an effort to include your other half in your spur of the moment expeditions; try to explain your inspirations in words, and you'll end up closer than ever.

Secrets of Success in 2021

You're not the materialistic type, Goat, so success for you tends to be a project that turns out just the way you want it, a lucky find at a car boot sale, or a happy get-together with family or friends. Yet, success in the conventional sense could be yours this year.

You've got a lot going for you. Your creative abilities and your habit of becoming completely absorbed in a task, if it captures your imagination, ensure that you can produce very fine work. You will stick with the project until it's complete too, as long as it holds your interest. These qualities meet the Ox requirements of 2021 perfectly, and if you continue to select tasks that enable you to work in this way, you will be amazed at the results. Fame and fortune – or at the very least wealth and respect – will find their way to you.

Just make sure you guard against that *other* habit though, Goat. Inspiration strikes so often that you tend to abandon a half-finished masterpiece when an even grander vision grabs your attention. Like a true mountain-goat, you want to leap ever upwards pursuing more and more wonderful creations. This is very worthy, no doubt, but not ideal in an Ox year. This year, discipline is the difference between success and failure. *Complete* each task you set yourself, unless there is a very compelling, practical reason to put it aside.

The only other challenges likely to cause recurring difficulties, this year, are the unreasonable people destined to cross your path. They can't help it, Goat. They're walking manifestations of the invisible friction caused by the fact that the Ox is a water creature while the Goat belongs to the fire family. Your basic elements just don't mix, and a lot of hissing steam is likely to result.

You'll be reminded of this whenever some normally rational person decides to throw a tantrum over nothing at all. Or that's how it'll seem to you. Some signs would simply shrug and ignore them, but being a sensitive Goat, you're likely to feel upset. Try to grow another skin, Goat, and don't allow them to throw you off course. It's not their fault and, chances are, they don't even mean it; don't take their attitude personally, and keep doing what you're doing.

The Goat Year at a Glance

January – Hangovers all round as the year opens. If you didn't overdo it, Goat, tiptoe about and cheer everyone up. They need positive you to inspire them.

February – Your finances are recovering from the Christmas splurge. Try to stash away any spare cash. You're going to want to treat yourself later.

March – Uh, oh. Lock up your credit cards. Some very tempting purchase has caught your eye. Wait before you commit yourself.

April – Work is going well. Authority figures are intrigued. Dress to impress.

May – Interesting encounters in your social life could lead to romance. Don't let your heart rule your head, though.

June – A green-eyed colleague is feeling resentful. Ignore hurtful comments. They're jealous.

July – A well-deserved pay rise or windfall is heading your way. Maybe you can treat yourself now.

August – Social stars are blazing bright, and you're invited to everything. Romance looks exciting.

September – You've been so popular, you've aroused envy again. Keep a low profile while you enjoy your good fortune.

October – Cash is rolling in, and you're feeling wonderful. Shower your loved ones with goodies.

November – Work is going from strength to strength, don't slacken off even though the holidays are near.

December – You're ready to party. Enjoy the celebrations but try not to be too extravagant. You'll need some cash next year.

Lucky colors for 2021: Gold, chocolate

Lucky numbers for 2021: 8, 2

CHAPTER 9: THE MONKEY

Monkey Years

6 February 1932 – 25 January 1933

25 January 1944 – 12 February 1945

12 February 1956 – 30 January 1957

30 January 1968 – 16 February 1969

16 February 1980 – 4 February 1981

4 February 1992 – 22 January 1993

22 January 2004 – 8 February 2005

8 February 2016 – 27 January 2017

26 January 2028 – 12 February 2029

Natural Element: Metal

Will 2021 be a Golden year for the Monkey?

Whoop, whoop! You might like to throw a few somersaults or leap over a gate, Monkey, because 2021 is set to be a brilliant year!

If you're typical of your sign, you shouldn't have come out of 2020 too badly, all things considered. As long as you and your loved ones stayed well, even the lockdown shouldn't have been too tedious, as your inventive Monkey brain is never short of intriguing ideas with which to entertain yourself and anyone who happens to be in your orbit.

What's more, since you belong to the metal family of creatures, last year's ruling metal element would have suited you perfectly. And that's why this Ox year should prove even better for you – because 2021 also happens to be a metal year, so you'll fit right in from day one.

Plus, there's the added bonus of your happy relationship with the King of the year, the mighty Ox. Although essentially a serious-minded beast, the Ox is surprisingly fond of the Monkey despite your cheeky ways. So, thanks to the Ox's indulgent attitude to everything primate, you can expect to find that your endeavors – whatever they happen to be – tend to meet with approval and support this year.

The only slightly tricky aspect to the brew is that the Ox is a water creature. This is good in one way as water and metal elements are believed to be harmonious and work well together, but the drawback in the partnership is that metal is thought to be nurturing to water. This is another reason why Ox is fond of you Monkey – Ox feels supported when a metal creature is around and will sometimes call on you to provide that support. But it's likely you won't find the arrangement quite so enjoyable.

This type of energy could play out in your daily life as frequent appeals to help out at home and at work. If you're not careful, you could wear yourself out running around on endless family mercy missions or rescuing your colleagues from silly mistakes at work.

Fortunately, you're so clever you're easily capable of saving the day, but you need to pace yourself to prevent burnout.

The compensation for all this is that the cash is rolling in for you, Monkey, and your ventures are blessed. The Ox demands that you approach your career with discipline and integrity – which might make you sigh at times because you're highly skilled at cutting corners and noticing shortcuts that others overlook – but stick to the rules, humor the Ox, and the sky could be the limit for you.

Monkeys whose jobs came to an end during last year's upheavals needn't worry. This could well be the moment to put your creative abilities to good use and launch that business or freelance idea that's been germinating at the back of your mind for a while. This would be risky right now for many signs, but you are especially favored. As long as you do your homework, pay attention to the fine print, and plan the details carefully, you could be surprised at how well it goes.

Employed Monkeys can expect the boss to be particularly appreciative this year. In difficult, unpredictable times, your flexible, quick-thinking approach is exactly what the company needs. Play your cards right, and you can make yourself indispensable. Promotion and pay rises will follow.

And with all this cash washing around, quite a few Monkeys will be considering a house move this year and looking at property. As a restless sign, the Monkey likes a frequent change of scenery. Yet, in a way, the search is more appealing to the novelty-seeking Monkey brain than an actual change of address. Monkey loves poking around all manner of different homes and exploring new neighborhoods, each more intriguing than the next.

You particularly enjoy a project, and can spot a thousand inventive ways to improve and redesign a property, though you don't necessarily want to do the work yourself. Many a Monkey will be sketching new layouts and measuring up for furniture – even checking the cost of renovations. Yet, somehow, once the possibilities have been thoroughly explored, Monkey is off to see the next contender, just in case it's a little better.

Chances are, most primates will arrive in 2022 with dozens of delightful property visits under their belts, but no new home.

On the other hand, should you happen to come across the perfect place, the Ox will help smooth the way for a brand new Monkey homestead.

What it Means to be a Monkey

There was a time when we tended to regard the Monkey as a figure of fun. The creature's awesome agility, effortless acrobatics, and natural clowning made us laugh, and if they sensed an audience, the animals would show off shamelessly. Which, of course, only made us enjoy them more.

Yet, in China, the Monkey was credited with far more qualities than merely those of a born entertainer. The sign of the Monkey is associated with intelligence, justice, and wisdom. Behind those mischievous eyes, the Chinese detected a shrewd brain and ability to plan the best course of action.

Like their namesakes, people born under the sign of Monkey tend to be physically agile. They're quick-moving, quick-thinking types with glittering wit and charismatic personalities. At a party, the Monkey will be in the centre of the group that's convulsed with laughter. Monkeys love jokes and humour of all kinds, and if anyone's going to start entertaining the crowd with a few magic tricks, it's likely to be a Monkey.

While not necessarily conventionally good-looking, the Monkey's lively face and sparkling eyes are always attractive, and Monkeys have no difficulty in acquiring partners. The tricky bit for a Monkey is staying around long enough to build a relationship.

People born under this sign need constant mental stimulation. They don't necessarily expect others to provide it. They are quite happy to amuse themselves with puzzles, conundrums, the mending of broken objects, and inventing things, but they also need new places and new faces. Few signs can keep up with Monkey's constant motion.

What's more, Monkeys are not good with rules or authority. They've seldom seen a rule that they don't want to break or avoid. In fact, it sometimes seems as if Monkey deliberately seeks out annoying regulations just for the fun of finding a way around them.

Yet, beneath the humour and games, the Monkey is ambitious with an astute brain. Monkeys can turn their hand to almost anything and make a success of it, but they're probably best-suited to working for themselves. If anyone is going to benefit from their efforts they believe it should be, chiefly, themselves. Also, they're not good at taking orders and, to be fair, they're so clever they don't need to. They can usually see the best way to carry out a task better than anyone else.

The Monkey home is often a work in progress. Monkey is always looking for a quicker, easier, cheaper, or more efficient way of doing everything and new ideas could encompass the entire building from the plumbing to the lighting and novel security systems. The first home in the street to be operated by remote control is likely to be the Monkey's. Yet, chances are, Monkey would prefer to meet friends in a nearby restaurant.

When it comes to holidays, Monkeys can have a bag packed seemingly in seconds, and are ready to be off anywhere, anytime. They don't much mind where they go as long as it's interesting, unusual, and offers plenty to be discovered. Lying on a sun-lounger for extended periods does not appeal.

Best Jobs for Monkey 2021

Dentist

Actor

Illusionist

Gymnast

Photojournalist

Game designer

Perfect Partners

Cupid's arrow can strike anywhere at any time, of course, but once the novelty of new romance wears off, some relationships are easier to maintain than others. Here's a guide to the Monkey compatibility with other signs.

Monkey with Monkey

It's not always the case that opposites attract. More often, like attracts like and when two Monkeys get together, they find each other delightful. At last, they've met another brain as quick and agile as their own and a person who relishes practical jokes as much as they do. What's more, this is a partner that shares a constant need for change and novelty. Yet, despite this, two Monkeys can often end up competing with each other. As long as they can recognise this, and laugh about it, they'll be fine.

Monkey with Rooster

While not a perfect match, these two have got a lot of time for each other. Monkey recognises the intelligent brain beneath Rooster's plumage while Rooster admires Monkey's ability to entertain a crowd and they both adore socialising. They could enjoy many fun dates together. Long-term, though, Rooster may tire of Monkey's jokes.

Monkey with Dog

Monkey finds Dog intriguing. Monkey senses Dog's strength of character coupled with its playful streak, which fits well with Monkey's love of games. Dog, meanwhile, appreciates Monkey's energy and light-hearted approach. Yet, before long, Monkey's disdain for rules will grate on Dog's instinctive love of them. They cannot agree in this area, and it could lead to arguments.

Monkey with Pig

On the surface, these two might seem an unlikely couple. Yet Pig enjoys Monkey's fun and humour while Monkey is happy to be admired uncritically. What's more, Monkey's inventive mind can solve any difficulties caused by Pig's spending and since Monkey can't resist a challenge, the opportunity to retrain Pig, or at least find a way to obtain purchases cheaper, could help the relationship last.

Monkey with Rat

Unlikely as it might appear, mischievous Monkey and the clever Rat make a good partnership. Their quick minds, sociable natures, and love of novelty ensure that they're never bored together. True, Rat might sometimes feel that Monkey is too inclined to skim over the surface of things and could do with being more serious at times, but Monkey's ingenuity and audaciousness always saves the day. Both can have a weakness for gambling though, so need to take care.

Monkey with Ox

The naughty Monkey scandalises Ox but in such an amusing way that Ox can't help laughing. Monkey, on the other hand, is equally amused to find an audience so easy to shock. This unlikely pair enjoy each other's company and get on surprisingly well. Yet, right from the start, it's probably obvious to both that a long-term relationship couldn't last. A fun flirtation, though, could be a terrific tonic for them both.

Monkey with Tiger

Tiger can't help being intrigued by sparkling Monkey and Monkey is flattered by such interest. Who wouldn't enjoy being admired by such a fabulous creature? But irrepressible Monkey just can't help teasing, and being teased is not a sensation Tiger is familiar with (or appreciates). Unless the attraction is very strong, these two will wind each other up until they can bear it no longer and part.

Monkey with Rabbit

Mercurial Monkey doesn't really 'get' Rabbit. The Monkey can appreciate how well Rabbit operates and sees this approach gets good results, but it's all too picky and slow for Monkey. Rabbit, on the other hand, is amused by Monkey's quick wit and clever ways but deplores Monkey's slapdash, sometimes devious tactics. Very unlikely to work out.

Monkey with Dragon

These two are likely to hit it off immediately. Each is attracted to the other's intelligence and lively presence, and Dragon's exuberance doesn't overwhelm hyperactive Monkey. What's more, although they both enjoy being surrounded by a crowd, Monkey only wants to make people laugh while Dragon hopes to inspire them to a cause. There is no conflict, so this couple can help each other to go far.

Monkey with Snake

These two clever creatures ought to admire each other, if only for their fine minds and, at first, it's possible they might. But unless they're really determined to make it work, it won't be long before active Monkey finds Snake's energy-saving ways irritating, while Snake loses patience with Monkey's endless jokes.

Monkey with Horse

Uh oh – best not attempted unless it's love at first sight. Monkey and Horse have wildly different outlooks and can't seem to see eye to eye on anything. They're both lively but in different ways that don't complement each other. Monkey will consider Horse's moods illogical and pointless while Horse is irritated that Monkey makes no attempt to understand how Horse feels. Very hard work.

Monkey with Goat

Monkey and Goat are different but in a good way. Though they don't quite 'get' each other deep down, Goat admires Monkey's lively personality and magical ability to come up with solutions for everything, while curious Monkey enjoys Goat's knowledge of the arts and the unusual. Long-term, Goat might not present enough of a challenge for Monkey but, with effort, it's a promising match.

Monkey Love 2021 Style

The typical Monkey loves to socialize, so last year's isolated lockdowns could have been frustrating. With this in mind, both single and attached Monkeys intend to make up for lost time in 2021. As long as there are no mass gathering bans near the Monkey pad, it's party central Chez Primate.

You're always popular, Monkey, but with Ox cheering you on, you're more in demand than ever. Single Monkeys will glide from admirer to admirer and back again with ease. And should you find yourself barred from meeting in person, you'll come up with some intriguing games online. There could be a lot of dressing up, clowning around, and raiding the make-up box for the camera, to make everyone laugh.

In fact, single Monkeys will be so appealing and such a tonic, the other signs just can't help falling in love. Many a Monkey could end up fielding more than one marriage proposal in 2021. Yet, just like the new home situation, this year quite a few primates will prefer checking out the possibilities to actually committing and settling down.

The Ox, however, likes to see romance completed with a proper home and even better, a family on the way, so if you should find a new love particularly enticing, Monkey, wedding bells could easily follow.

Attached Monkeys and their partners are out for fun, and as long as your other half is as wild and energetic as you, the two of you will have a ball. It's difficult to keep up with you though, Monkey, so if you want the relationship to last you need to be considerate. A few early nights and a curb on flirting with everyone you see, when you're out together, will work wonders.

Secrets of Success in 2021

You've got everything you need to reach your goals this year, Monkey; opportunities, support, friendly faces, even access to cash if you need it. Thanks to the benevolent help from the Ox, your path will be smoothed wherever possible.

The only thing that could hold you back is your own judgement. You're so versatile and clever you can make a success of many different occupations and – this year – you're likely to be showered with tempting offers. There's a danger you could take on too much or accept too many roles because you're unable to turn down an exciting proposition.

Bearing in mind the additional calls for help you're likely to encounter in 2021, it will be all too easy to find you quickly become overloaded and worn out.

You think you can juggle everything, Monkey, but you can't. Not if you intend to make it into 2022 in good shape.

So, in 2021, your secret of success is to think: 'Less is more.' Choose just a few choice projects, stick with them, and disregard the rest.

The Monkey Year at a Glance

January – The year gets off to a great start. You can feel the atmosphere changing.

February – Already you're starting to be flavor of the month. Check out a job offer heading your way.

March – Someone is looking at you with envious eyes. Not surprising, but is it a colleague or a new love? Maybe they want your attention, not your cash.

April – An authority figure suddenly notices your talents. Be on your best behavior now. Act responsibly. This is not the time for practical jokes.

May – A cash windfall has your name on it. Don't gamble the farm but a little flutter you can afford might pay off.

June – Time to burn off some of that nervous energy. You often forget how much you need a workout. Put your career on the back burner and think exercise.

July – If you've got a new fitness routine in place, now's the time to brush up those career skills. Mind and body in harmony.

August – Romance is blossoming around you. You could be juggling two admirers. Enjoy but make sure they don't meet.

September – A good time to take a late holiday if you haven't been away yet.

October – Work is gathering pace. You're getting busier and busier. Pace yourself.

November – You've attracted attention again at work. You may even be head-hunted. Consider all offers very carefully.

December – Family is in the mood to party for once. Relatives, once at loggerheads, seem to have settled their scores. Enjoy the peace.

Lucky colors for 2021: Orange, Silver, Red, White

Lucky numbers for 2021: 9, 2, 5

CHAPTER 10: THE ROOSTER

Rooster Years

26 January 1933 – 13 February 1934

13 February 1945 – 1 February 1946

31 January 1957 – 17 February 1958

17 February 1969 – 5 February 1970

5 February 1981 – 24 January 1982

23 January 1993 – 9 February 1994

9 February 2005 – 28 January 2006

28 January 2017 – 15 February 2018

13 February 2029 – 2 February 2030

Natural Element: Metal

Will 2021 be a Golden Year for the Rooster?

So, Rooster, how are you feeling? Do you get the sense you're on the verge of something big? Even if you're not quite sure what it is? Well, if you do, your instincts are spot on because 2021 is the year you're destined to make things happen.

Last year probably didn't turn out the way you thought it might, yet strangely, as long as you and your loved ones remained healthy, chances are you didn't find the confining atmosphere too unbearable. The truth is that although Roosters have a fine pair of wings and enjoy their share of flying around, they actually prefer to stay fairly close to home.

The enforced lockdown may have had its frustrations – the typical Rooster will have missed the chance to get dressed up and strut about attracting admiring glances – but deep down you will have secretly enjoyed the excuse to step back, take a break, and savor the chance to plan your next adventure at a leisurely pace.

And now, with the arrival of the Year of the Ox, you're almost ready to make a major move. It doesn't matter if you're still undecided about the direction you want to take. This year, you're on the brink, and by the time 2022 comes around, you'll have got things sorted.

One of the reasons the Year of the Ox is favorable for you, Rooster, is because (unlikely as it sounds) in many ways you and the Ox are two of a kind. You're both farm creatures. You both like the security of a settled base and though you may appear to be extrovert and showy – on the surface – the Ox understands that beneath those fine feathers you're sensitive and serious. Just like the Ox, in fact.

So, Ox has a lot of time for Roosters, and will assist you where possible.

Then there's the fact that 2021 is another Metal year. Like the Monkey before you, and the Dog which comes after, the Rooster belongs to the Metal family of zodiac animals, so you're immediately on the right wavelength for the times. You instinctively understand the zeitgeist of the year, so any inspirations that strike in the next 12 months are likely to be well received.

What's more, the Ox is a Water creature which is also helpful. In the Chinese cycle, Metal is believed to nurture Water, so the Ox feels supported when Rooster's around, and the Rooster feels appreciated in Ox's company.

This could play out very happily in day-to-day life, as promotions all round at work for employed Roosters. Roosters are excellent managers, but their confidence is easily dented and, in less favorable years, this can lead to their talent being overlooked. With the support of the Ox in 2021, though, things are different. Now the hard-working Rooster can bask in well-deserved appreciation, and if you're not already in a management role, it won't be long before you're offered one.

Self-employed Roosters, and Roosters with their own businesses, can expect the respect they inspire to grow and grow and their services become ever more in demand. In fact, it could reach the stage where you have to turn work away because you just can't cope with it all.

And with so much good career news around, it won't be long before increased cash begins pouring into the Rooster coffers. Naturally, if you're a typical Rooster, you'll immediately start thinking about splurging on a flash new car, some designer clothes, or maybe even an impressive new home. Well, if you're certain you can afford it, Rooster, go for it. But just remember that not all years are as favorable for you as this one; it wouldn't hurt to put a little aside for leaner times.

Yet, beneath all the excitement, there is something else going on for many Roosters. You're building up to a big change. The preparations started last year on some level, even it was just deep down in your subconscious. Now, the impetus is gathering pace. You're drawn to making some meaningful improvements to your life and, as the year goes on, the right destination for you will become clearer.

Whether you change your career, start a new business, move to a different town, city, or maybe the depths of the countryside, or completely reorganize your social scene, you're gearing up for a big overhaul. It could take 12 months to achieve, but chances are, by the time 2022 comes around, your life will look very different – in a good way!

What it means to be a Rooster

Colorful, bold, and distinctly noisy, the Rooster rules the farmyard. Seemingly fearless and relishing the limelight, this bird may be small, but he doesn't appear to know it. We're looking at a giant personality here. This creature may be the bane of late sleepers, and only a fraction of the size of other animals on the farm, but the Rooster doesn't care. Rooster struts around, puffing out his tiny chest as if he owns the place.

The Chinese associate the Rooster with courage, and it's easy to see why. You'd have to be brave to square up to all-comers armed only with a modest beak, a couple of sharp claws, and a piercing shriek. Yet, Rooster is quite prepared to take on the challenge.

People born in the year of the Rooster tend to be gorgeous to look at, and like to dress flamboyantly. Even if their physique is not as slender as it could be, the Rooster is not going to hide it away in drab, black outfits. Roosters enjoy colour and style, and they dress to be noticed. These are not shy retiring types. They like attention, and they do whatever they can to get it.

Roosters are charming and popular with quick minds and engaging repartee. They have to guard against a tendency to boast, but this happens mainly when they sense a companion's interest is wandering. And since they're natural raconteurs, they can usually recapture attention and pass their stories off as good entertainment.

Like the feathered variety, Roosters can be impetuous and impulsive. They tend to rush into situations and commitments that are far too demanding, without a second thought and then, later on, wonder frantically how they're going to manage. Oddly enough, they usually make things work but only after ferocious effort. Roosters just can't help taking a risk.

Although they're gregarious and often surrounded by friends, there's a sense that – deep down – few people know the real Rooster. Underneath the bright plumage and cheerful banter, Rooster is quite private and a little vulnerable. Perhaps Roosters fear they'll disappear or get trampled on if they don't make enough noise. So they need frequent reassurance that they're liked and appreciated.

With all the emphasis Rooster puts on the splendid Rooster appearance, it's often overlooked that, in fact, the Rooster has a good brain and is quite a thinker. Roosters keep up with current affairs, they're shrewd with money and business matters, and though you never see them doing it, in private they're busily reading up on all the latest information on their particular field.

At work, Rooster wants to be the boss and often ends up that way. Failing that, Roosters will go it alone and start their own business. They're usually successful due to the Rooster's phenomenal hard work, but when things do go wrong, it's likely to be down to the Rooster's compulsion to take a risk or promise more than it's possible to deliver. Also, while being sensitive to criticism, themselves, Roosters can be extremely frank in putting across their views to others. They may pride themselves on their plain-speaking, but it may not do them any favours with customers and employees.

Rooster thinks the home should be a reflection of its owner's splendid image so, if at all possible, it will be lavish, smart, and full of enviable items. They have good taste, in a colourful way, and don't mind spending money on impressive pieces. If the Rooster can be persuaded to take a holiday, a five-star hotel in a prestigious location with plenty of socialising would be ideal, or a luxury cruise with a place at the Captain's Table.

Best Jobs for Rooster

Catwalk Model

Dress designer

Air steward

Chef

Swimming Instructor

TV Presenter

Personal Trainer

Perfect Partners

Cupid's arrow can strike anywhere at any time, of course, but once the novelty of new romance wears off, some relationships are easier to maintain than others. Here's a guide to the Rooster's compatibility with other signs.

Rooster with Rooster

Fabulous to look at though they would be, these two alpha creatures would find it difficult to share the limelight. They can't help admiring each other at first sight, but since both needs to be the boss, there could be endless squabbles for dominance. What's more, neither would be able to give the other the regular reassurance they need. Probably not worth attempting.

Rooster with Dog

Rooster and Dog are not the best of partners. Dog can be as plain-spoken as Rooster and is not likely to be impressed by overt show. What's more, Dog is often critical, and Rooster can't stand criticism. Rooster, on the other hand, is likely to sense and resent Dog's attitude. Frustration abounds for both in this relationship. Only for the hopelessly love-struck.

Rooster with Pig

These two might seem an unlikely couple – modest Pig with extrovert Rooster. Yet Pig has no need or wish to crow and can see the vulnerable character that lurks beneath Rooster's fine feathers; Rooster, meanwhile, responds to Pig's kindness and undemanding nature. As long as Rooster doesn't get bored, this can be a contented relationship.

Rooster with Rat

The first thing Rat notices about the Rooster is its beautiful plumage, but this is a relationship which is unlikely to get much further than initial admiration. Rooster's direct and frank approach can strike the Rat as tactless, while the Rooster can't understand why Rat has to make life so convoluted and complicated. Then again, Rooster's natural confidence and aplomb can come across as bragging to the Rat. These two have to be very determined to make a partnership work.

Rooster with Ox

For all its bravado and showing off, the Rooster is a down-to-earth type, drawn to security and accumulating the good things in life – requirements that Ox understands very well and can supply effortlessly. What's more, Ox can't help but admire Rooster's fine feathers and skill at communicating in a crowd – attributes Ox doesn't have and is unlikely to acquire. These two could enjoy a very good partnership.

Rooster with Tiger

The only feathered creature in the zodiac, the opulence and novelty of Rooster's appearance will draw Tiger like a magnet. What's more, deep down they are both quite serious-minded types so on one level they'll have much to share. Yet, despite this, they're not really on the same wavelength and misunderstandings will keep recurring. Could be hard work.

Rooster with Rabbit

A difficult match. However unfair it seems, Rooster comes over as loud, boastful, and uncouth to Rabbit while Rabbit appears dull, staid, and insufficiently admiring of Rooster's fine feathers to appeal to Rooster. These two just can't see below the surface of the other and it would be surprising if they ended up together. Only to be considered by the very determined.

Rooster with Dragon

A Dragon and Rooster pairing will always attract attention. These two are both gorgeous beings and love to be surrounded by admirers. They will probably enjoy going out together and being seen as a couple, but in the long-term they may not be able to provide the kind of support each secretly needs. Entertaining for a while but probably not a lasting relationship.

Rooster with Snake

Surprisingly, Snake and Rooster work well together. Both gorgeous in different ways, they complement each other without competing. Snake's keen eyes can see beneath Rooster's proud facade to the sensitive, unsure person inside, while Rooster appreciates Snake's unobtrusive strength and wise words of encouragement at just the right moment. These two could be inseparable.

Rooster with Horse

The eye-catching Rooster intrigues Horse while Rooster appreciates Horse's strength and agility. They can enjoy many stimulating dates together. Yet, in the long-run, this couple may not be able to provide the stability the other needs. They're both sensitive types but in different ways. After a while, the relationship could run out of steam.

Rooster with Goat

Peaceful Goat is not one to make feathers fly, so these two are unlikely to fall out, but they're unlikely to find perfect compatibility either. Goat is unable to give Rooster the regular ego boosts that make Rooster thrive while Rooster is baffled by Goat's unpredictable devotion to impractical projects or people. Misunderstandings are likely.

Rooster with Monkey

While not a perfect match, these two have got a lot of time for each other. Monkey recognises the intelligent brain beneath Rooster's plumage while Rooster admires Monkey's ability to entertain a crowd and they both adore socialising. They could enjoy many fun dates together. Long-term, though, Rooster may tire of Monkey's jokes.

Rooster Love 2021 Style

You have to admit that Roosters have a certain reputation where romance is concerned. Like your unassuming cousin, the Rabbit, people tend to believe you're not exactly picky when it comes to partners. Maybe it's something to do with your splendid looks, colorful clothes, and the way you take such obvious pride in showing them off, but onlookers make the mistake of thinking this display is all about attracting new lovers. They couldn't be more wrong. They fail to see the Rooster loves dressing up just for the sheer fun of it.

Yet though attracting attention may not be your sole aim, Rooster, this year you'll be fighting off potential partners. Your fine feathers are getting you noticed like never before, and you might even have to fend off some unwelcome advances. They simply don't get that, actually, you are very discerning about relationships. It takes a special kind of person to earn your trust.

Single Roosters might have to use those wings to escape admirers who won't take no for an answer. Yet, somewhere amongst the crowd, there could be the 'one', so don't be too hasty with the brush-offs Rooster.

Attached Roosters will find their partner rediscovering their charms all over again. This could be a very happy time in the homestead. With a little thought, you could deepen your relationship and take it to a new level, especially if you share with your partner those hopes for enhancing your life. Build a joint dream together, and this could be one of your best years yet.

Secrets of Success

Doing well should come easily to you this year, Rooster, thanks to the Ox's help behind the scenes. People in authority are noticing you, and all you have to do is keep believing in yourself and working conscientiously.

You can have too much of a good thing, though. You're likely to become so sought after that there's a temptation to take on more than you can handle. Respect often means more to you than hard cash, and when there's so much appreciation and praise headed your way, you tend to get so intoxicated with delight that you feel superhuman.

Trouble is, you're not. In fact, energetic as you often appear, the Rooster constitution is not as robust as it seems. You need to pace yourself; stop and take a break before you get tired, not after. Resist all pleas to fit in just one more task when your schedule is full.

And of course, as always, fight the urge to give everyone who'll listen to a blow-by-blow account of your string of successes or your latest list of expensive purchases. You don't mean to boast – you're just so exuberant you want to share your happy news – but that's not how most other people will interpret it. Some will be jealous, while others will think you're bragging. Not a good look either way, Rooster. Just don't go there!

The Rooster Year at a Glance

January – Strength is returning. After a nerve-wracking few months, you're ready for action.

February – Opportunities are beginning to flow. This is only the start, Rooster, so you can afford to be picky.

March – Authority figures are warming to you, but this could make others envious. Keep your head down, and your words modest, but enjoy the praise secretly.

April – Perhaps it's spring, but your mind is bursting with exciting plans. Write down even your craziest of ideas. Your inspirations could turn to gold later this year.

May – The boss could suggest a pay rise or a new role, and romance is in the air. Don't work so long you haven't got time for dating.

June – Another week, another opportunity it seems. Those offers are turning into a flood. You can't do it all, Rooster. Accept the ones that line up with your long-term goals.

July – The heat's rising and colleagues and friends are talking holidays. Chances are you're too busy right now. Plan some weekends away or outdoor picnics.

August – You really could take a break now, Rooster. You can afford to allow yourself a week or two away. Go for it.

September – Temptations to splurge are all around. You do love pretty things. Spoil yourself if you're quite sure you can afford it.

October – You're feeling confident and ready to take a gamble. Think very carefully, Rooster. Check every angle. Don't waste money.

November – Those long-term plans are taking shape in a pleasing way. Keep on doing what you're doing, Rooster.

December – Looks like you could be planning a big Christmas party. There's a lot to celebrate. Finally, you can show off all your beautiful new toys. Give yourself a well-earned pat on the back.

Lucky colors 2021: Purple, White, Orange

Lucky numbers 2021: 1, 8

CHAPTER 11: THE DOG

Dog Years

14 February 1934 – 3 February 1935

2 February 1946 – 21 January 1947

18 February 1958 – 7 February 1959

6 February 1970 – 26 January 1971

25 January 1982 – 12 February 1983

10 February 1994 – 30 January 1995

29 January 2006 – 17 February 2007

16 February 2018 – 4 February 2019

Natural Element: Metal

Will 2021 be a Golden Year for the Dog?

Congratulations, Dog. You've successfully negotiated what turned out to be a very tricky year, and can now look forward to an easier, much less nerve-wracking time in 2021 – the 12 months ruled by the Golden Ox.

Last year, the Golden Rat was in charge of course, and in theory it should have been a promising year for you, as you and the Rat get on pretty well. The only problem with this combination is that you tend to be a born worrier; you like to know where you stand at all times, and you prefer a sense of security. The Rat, on the other hand, couldn't care less about such concerns and loves the thrill of change and adventure.

In normal times, you can cope with this mismatch by keeping calm and avoiding too much risky behavior, but 2020 was not normal by any stretch of the imagination. In 2020, the Rat's instinct for change went into hyperdrive, and it was very difficult for any of the signs to keep up. Yet somehow, despite moments of panic, most Dogs managed to hang on in there. You may have acquired a few more grey hairs, but chances are, you've learned a lot and will now be able to profit from some of those tough lessons.

The good news is that the Golden Ox ushers in the sort of conditions that suit you best, Dog. The Ox slows things down and gives everyone a chance to attend to the details and start rebuilding or repairing anything that came adrift in the whirlwind that was the Rat's progress.

You can get your breath back now, and start sorting out the direction you want to take. Because you're probably beginning to realize that you reached a crossroads last year; maybe it was a crossroads you didn't even realize was there. Yet as 2021 begins, you can see quite clearly that you *don't want* things to continue in the same old way. The moment has come to move forward with big improvements in mind, and this year you will get the chance to transform your lifestyle.

Like last year, the ruling element the Ox brings in is metal, which suits you just fine as the Dog belongs to the metal family of animals. Deep down, you understand the mood of the year, and you can work with it.

The other encouraging aspect is your relationship with the Ox. You and the Ox – while not being total besties – get on amicably together. Ox respects the Dog and approves of your conscientious, loyal approach, while the Dog completely understands and supports the Ox's phenomenal work ethic and refusal to abandon a task until it is complete.

For this reason, any career projects you undertake this year, Dog, are likely to fly. The Ox is supporting you all the way. Employed Dogs will find their employers unusually helpful and appreciative. Freelance and self-employed Dogs will be more in demand than ever. And Dogs that are considering taking the plunge, and starting new ventures, will find doors that were previously shut fast beginning to swing open.

Yet many Dogs will be planning something completely new. There's a good chance you may move home this year or at least start a serious search for the perfect place. And it's very likely that, along with your new home, you'll organize a new career too. You may well find yourself working from home – by choice – not because lockdown has forced you into it.

There's also the happy possibility that your family will be expanding in a very pleasing way. All Dogs enjoy more puppies on the scene and sooner or later most Dogs will find themselves surrounded by little ones. Whether it's a new addition to your own household, or the household of someone close to you, chances are your playful skills will be regularly required and admired.

You could even find yourself expanding further still and taking on an additional pet or two. The more the merrier as far as most Dogs are concerned; the new additions will bring you much joy.

In fact, many Dogs will be inspired to organize some sort of big family holiday or get-together of the generations to celebrate. Indoor venues may still be difficult, but most Dogs prefer to be in the open air anyway; so think fun and games in the countryside or a big beach BBQ, and you'll be in your element.

It would also be a good idea to add a new exercise regime to this year's to-do list while you're organizing your fresh start, Dog. This isn't simply to keep in shape. You need to be physically fit because there's a chance you could be called upon to come to the rescue, in some way, more than once this year. This is because while the Dog belongs to the metal family of creatures, the Ox is a water beast.

The elements of metal and water are believed to work harmoniously together, so this is good news for people born under these signs. The only potential downside for the metal family is that metal is thought to be supportive and nurturing of water. This means the metals are likely to be called upon, quite frequently, for that support when a water creature is in charge of the year. In the case of Dogs, famous for their rescue skills, this tendency could actually play out in the form of regular requests for actual physical aid.

Whether it's picking up stranded motorists, taking in a flooded out neighbor, patching up a walker with a sprained ankle, or simply rescuing a cat from a tree, you could find yourself answering quite a few SOSs this year. Yet, surprisingly, where other signs might sigh in irritation, you're more likely to glow with pride. The typical Dog comes into its own when being of service to others. You're likely to find this a most satisfying year.

What it means to be a Dog

Though some cultures are quite rude about the dog, and regard the very name as a disparaging term, in the West, we tend to be rather sentimental about our canine friends.

The Chinese, on the other hand, while regarding the zodiac Dog with respect, discern more weighty qualities in the faithful hound. They regard the sign of the Dog as representing justice and compassion.

People born under the sign of the Dog, therefore, are admired for their noble natures and fair-minded attitudes.

Typical Dogs will do the right thing, even if it means they'll lose out personally. They have an inbuilt code of honour that they hate to break.

The Dog is probably the most honest sign of the zodiac. People instinctively trust the Dog even if they don't always agree with Dog's opinions. Yet Dogs are usually completely unaware of the high esteem in which they're held, because they believe they're only acting naturally; doing what anyone else would do in the circumstances.

Since they have such a highly-developed sense of right and wrong, Dogs understand the importance of rules. Also, since deep down they're always part of a pack – even if it's invisible – Dogs know that fairness is vital. If there aren't fair shares all round, there's likely to be trouble they believe. So, to keep the peace, Dog knows that a stout framework of rules is required and once set up, everyone should stick to them. Dogs are genuinely puzzled that other signs can't seem to grasp this simple truth!

People born under this sign tend to be physically strong with thick, glossy hair, and open, friendly faces. Their warm manner attracts new acquaintances, but they tend to stay acquaintances for quite a while. It takes a long time for Dog to promote a person from acquaintance to real friend. This is because Dogs are one hundred percent loyal and will never let a friend down, so they don't give their trust lightly.

Dogs are intelligent and brave, and once they've made up their mind, they stick to it. They're quite prepared to go out on a limb for a good cause if necessary, but they don't really like being alone. They're much happier in a group, with close friends or family. What's more, though they're good managers, they're not interested in being in overall charge. They'd much rather help someone else achieve a goal than take all the responsibility themselves.

At work, Dog can be a puzzle to the boss. Though capable of immense effort, and obviously the dedicated type, it's difficult to enthuse the Dog. Promises of pay rises and promotion have little effect. The Dog is just not materialistic or particularly ambitious in the conventional sense. Yet, if a crisis appears, if someone's in trouble or disaster threatens, the Dog is suddenly energised and springs into action. In fact, it's quite difficult to hold Dog back. Dogs will work tirelessly, without rest or thought of reward, until the rescue is achieved.

Bearing this in mind, Dogs would do well to consider a career that offers some kind of humanitarian service. This is their best chance of feeling truly fulfilled and happy at work.

At home, Dogs have a down to earth approach. Home and stability are very important to them. They're not the types to keep moving and trading up, but at the same time, they don't need their home to be a showcase. The Dog residence will be comfortable rather than stylish with the emphasis on practicality. Yet, it will have a warm, inviting atmosphere, and the favoured visitors permitted to join the family there will be certain of a friendly welcome.

It's not easy to get Dog to take a break if there's a cause to be pursued, but when Dogs finally allow themselves to come off-duty, they love to play. They like to be out in the open air or splashing through water, and can discover their competitive streak when it comes to team games.

Best Jobs for Dog

Store detective

Nursery Manager

Teacher

Police Officer

Ambulance Driver

Fire Fighter

Charity Boss

Kennel Manager

Perfect Partners

Cupid's arrow can strike anywhere at any time, of course, but once the novelty of new romance wears off, some relationships are easier to maintain than others. Here's a guide to the Dog compatibility with other signs.

Dog with Dog

Dogs love company so these two will gravitate to each other and stay there. Both loyal, faithful types, neither need worry the other will stray. They'll appreciate their mutual respect for doing things properly and their shared love of a stable, caring home. This relationship is likely to last and last. The only slight hitch could occur if, over time, the romance dwindles and Dog and Dog become more like good friends than lovers.

Dog with Pig

In the outside world, the Dog and the Pig can get along well together; in fact, Pigs being intelligent creatures can do many of the things dogs can do, so it's not surprising this zodiac pair make a good couple. Good-natured Pig is uncomplicated and fair-minded which suits Dog perfectly. Also, Pig brings out Dog's playful side – which delights Pig who's always keen to have a playmate. A happy relationship involving many restaurants.

Dog with Rat

The Rat and the Dog get along pretty well together. Both strong characters, they respect each other and give each other space when required. But deep down, the Dog is a worrier and gets anxious about unnecessary risks, while Rat just can't help sailing close to the wind if an interesting opportunity presents itself. Long-term, reckless Rat might unintentionally drive Dog to distraction. Only to be considered by Dogs with nerves of steel.

Dog with Ox

These two ought to get along well as they're both sensible, down to earth, loyal, and hardworking, and in tune with each other's basic beliefs. And yet, somehow they don't. Dog has a playful streak and finds this lacking in Ox, while Ox may be baffled by what seems like pointless silliness in Dog. If they can agree to differ, they could make a relationship work.

Dog with Tiger

While not exactly opposites, these two are different enough to intrigue each other yet similar enough in basic outlook to get on well. Both Tiger and Dog are idealistic and uninterested in material gain yet where Dog can be nervous, Tiger's bold. And where Tiger attracts controversy, Dog will be loyal. This partnership could be lasting and valuable.

Dog with Rabbit

Despite the fact that in the outside world Rabbit could easily end up as Dog's dinner, the astrological pair gets on surprisingly well. Dog appreciates Rabbit's careful, efficient ways and soft voice, while Rabbit admires Dog's energy and good intentions. Dog's lack of interest in the finer points of interior design might try Rabbit's patience, but with a little work, these two could reach an understanding.

Dog with Dragon

Not the easiest of combinations. Down-to-earth Dog can't see what all the fuss is about when it comes to Dragons. Unimpressed by glamour and irritated by what seems to Dog the gullibility of Dragon admirers, Dog can't be bothered to find out more. Dragon meanwhile, is hurt by Dog's lack of interest. Great determination would be needed to make this work.

Dog with Snake

Some snakes seem to have an almost hypnotic power, and for some reason, Dog is particularly susceptible to these skills. We've heard of snake-charmers, but snakes can be dog-charmers, and without even trying, Snakes can find themselves the recipients of Dog devotion. Since the Dog is strong, loyal, and can be fun, Snake is not averse to this but might, in the end, find it boring.

Dog with Horse

Both good friends of man, these two can make a formidable team. Dog understands the occasional need for solitude while admiring Horse's strength and agility. Horse, meanwhile, senses Dog's loyalty and down to earth nature. Both lovers of the great outdoors and physical activity, they'll never be short of adventures to share. A promising long-term relationship.

Dog with Goat

This is another relationship that could be tricky. Loyal Dog would be quite willing to stand by Goat when practical problems loom but could end up irritated by Goat's inability to learn from previous mistakes and so keeps making them. Goat can't understand why Dog gets so bothered. With care, these two could learn to live together.

Dog with Monkey

Monkey finds Dog intriguing. Monkey senses Dog's strength of character coupled with its playful streak, which fits well with Monkey's love of games. Dog, meanwhile, appreciates Monkey's energy and light-hearted approach. Yet before long, Monkey's disdain for rules will grate on Dog's instinctive love of them. They cannot agree in this area, and it could lead to arguments.

Dog with Rooster

Rooster and Dog are not the best of partners. Dog can be as plain-spoken as Rooster and is not likely to be impressed by overt show. What's more, Dog is often critical, and Rooster can't stand criticism. Rooster, on the other hand, is likely to sense and resent Dog's attitude. Frustration abounds for both in this relationship. Only for the hopelessly love-struck.

Dog Love 2021 Style

The unprecedented upheavals triggered by the Rat last year will have caused most signs to react in one of two ways – they're either out to party like crazy (to make up for lost time), or they'll be looking for security and permanence. Single Dogs tend to fall into the security section.

This year, idealistic single canines are looking for love. You've got no time for the flirty and insincere. Single Dogs want a proper soulmate to have fun with; to build something that lasts. One-night-standers need not apply. Even though you may not voice these thoughts, the vibes you're putting out will keep most chancers at bay. Yet, at the same time, you'll have a magnetic appeal for the many other signs who are looking for the same qualities as you.

Single Dogs can expect a string of interested potential lovers to cross their path in the next few months. There's no rush. You can afford to take things slowly and really get to know the ones who attract you most. By 2022, you could well find that your soulmate has arrived.

Attached Dogs are out to strengthen the foundations with their partner. This may take the form of actually rebuilding the family home or moving to a new one. Many Dogs will be welcoming new puppies into the pack and – this year – socializing with family and very close friends will be a top priority. Your shared bond will bring you closer together, and create great happiness.

Secrets of Success

Chances are, Dog, that although you enjoy cash flowing into your coffers, and are quite happy to win praise and promotion at work, you're not too bothered with conventional ideas of success. Particularly this year. You've always been a family-oriented person, and the trials and tribulations of 2020 have only reinforced your instincts that real success involves building a strong and healthy pack. So, it looks as if in 2021, most of your efforts will be directed towards reinforcing and expanding your foundations.

Despite this, your conscientious approach will be much appreciated professionally, and you're likely to do well without deliberately pushing yourself. Pay rises and promotions are a serious possibility. The only thing to guard against is your endearing habit of playfulness when you're feeling good. Family and friends find this charming and are only too happy to join in the fun and games... usually. But, at work, some of the dourer authority figures will not appreciate jokes or what they regard as silly behavior – even if previously they seemed to have more of a sense of humor.

This is down to the influence of the Ox. Last year's Rat was not averse to a bit of levity, so you could get away with some light-hearted fun in the workplace. Not so the Ox. Literal-minded Ox doesn't get it. Ox believes there's a time and a place for larking around – and it's not in a business setting. So, this year, remain strictly professional and correct at work, and you can't fail.

Finally, your biggest success could arise unexpectedly from some sort of rescue or charity event you find yourself caught up in. Unplanned and surprising, this bolt from the blue could really bowl you over. Recognition and even an award of some kind could follow.

The Dog Year at a Glance

January – It's back to work, but you've got some big ideas brewing. No need to rush. You've got 12 months to put them into action.

February – Looks like your boss is eyeing you up for extra responsibilities. Self-employed Dogs could be asked to take on more work. Say yes either way.

March – Spring is in the air. You can smell it. Don't take on so much you can't get out and socialize.

April – A bad-tempered grouch in your orbit is stomping around causing trouble. Ignore them if you can. If not... be diplomatic. Not your strong point, Dog, but try.

May – Accept an unusual invitation. Love could be lurking where you least expect it.

June – Romance in the open air brings good luck. Think picnics, riverside strolls, or starlight walks.

July – A neighbor or colleague calls for help. You're ready and willing to go to their aid. Follow your charitable instincts.

August – Looks like you could be holding the fort while everyone else takes a break. Don't stress it. You'll get a reward.

September – Praise all round for your efforts is gratifying, but could cause jealousy. Watch your back.

October – If there was no time for a holiday back in the summer, an autumn getaway could be ideal now.

November – Cash is flowing your way, Dog. If you feel like a splurge, now's the time.

December – A big family celebration is coming together. Watch out for a reckless relative who could cause friction, but don't forget to enjoy yourself!

Lucky colors for 2021: Scarlet, White, Yellow

Lucky numbers for 2021: 2, 5, 8

CHAPTER 12: THE PIG

Pig Years

4 February 1935 – 23 January 1936

22 January 1947 – 9 February 1948

8 February 1959 – 27 January 1960

27 January 1971 – 14 February 1972

13 February 1983 – 1 February 1984

31 January 1995 – 18 February 1996

18 February 2007 – 6 February 2008

5 February 2019 – 24 January 2020

Natural Element: Water

Will 2021 be a Golden Year for the Pig?

Okay, Pig, now would be a good moment to break out the chocolate biscuits, liberate your stash of crisps and nibbles, and settle down with a glass of prosecco or your favorite cocktail. It's time to say a not-so-fond farewell to the Rat who has run us all ragged throughout 2020, and welcome in the Ox in your own inimitable style.

Looking back over the past 12 months, it's clear that plenty of signs had a worse year than most Pigs. This is because, despite everything, the Rat is actually quite fond of you Pig and would have made things as easy for you as possible. This fact, coupled with your own generally laid-back temperament, will have helped you sail through various tense situations that would have caused serious grey hairs in other less relaxed creatures.

As long as you and your loved ones managed to remain well for the duration, the majority of Pigs should have reached 2021 in pretty good shape, if a little on the heavier side.

Yet, chances are, you're still disappointed at the way the decade started. Being forced to stay at home, shopping online, cut off from friends and all those delightful catch-ups over something tasty in a cozy restaurant was frustrating and sad; as was missing those joyous big celebrations for birthdays, weddings, and any other excuse for a party. That's not the Pig's idea of living life to the full.

Well, fortunately, 2021 is looking a lot better for Pigs. You are a popular sign and – like the Rat – the Ox is also fond of you. But, happily, the Ox expresses that fondness in a quieter, less dramatic way, and since an Ox year is – in any case – a calmer, less frenetic 12 months – the outcome should be much more satisfying to Pigs.

As difficult situations begin to settle down, you'll be able to emerge into your preferred way of life. Shopping and socializing can be resumed and many Pigs will be inspired to make up for lost time. In fact, you could find yourself going a bit wild this year, Pig.

You'll get away with it, too – up to a point. On your side, in addition to having the Ox in charge, is the fact that this is a metal year and you are a water sign. This is fortunate as metal is believed to nurture and assist water, so you'll be able to indulge in behavior that wouldn't be tolerated in other years.

Then again, the Ox is also a water sign, so on many levels, you're on the same wave-length and can flow along together quite amicably.

This means that in 2021 you'll be able to sail around obstacles in your path with unusual ease; awkward people will tend to float away without causing you too much trouble.

Metal represents money, so this metal year many Pigs will find cash showering into their lives, often unexpectedly. Surprise wins, insurance pay-outs, or work bonuses could delight the Pig homestead, and many Pigs will also make a profit selling off various household items unearthed during the lockdown.

The typical Pig home tends to be crammed with assorted treasures acquired during past expeditions but barely used since, and these could now bring in a very healthy sum. In fact, you really could find something very valuable in the attic. This is a win-win situation because selling on unused items simply makes room to acquire more stuff, along with the cash to purchase it. The Pig idea of bliss.

You may find, Pig, that your success in this direction inspires you to consider turning your sales skills into a new career, particularly if you find you now prefer to work from home.

If you do stay in your regular job, employed Pigs are set to be popular with everyone at work. Fortunately, the boss is in a receptive mood to most of the things you do, because many Pigs are more inclined to enjoy the workplace this year than get stuck into serious work. This goes for self-employed Pigs too. You're likely to crave company and find any excuse for a chat.

This won't hamper your progress right now as you're clever enough to make sure that – as well as socializing – you get just enough done to satisfy those in authority. It's probably not the best time though to aim too high promotion-wise.

This year, having fun is very important to most Pigs, and that usually involves a formidable amount of spending.

Having spent so much more time at home lately, many Pigs will have noticed endless ways they can improve their surroundings. Redecoration could be high on the agenda; new color schemes and furniture will naturally follow, and Pigs with outside space will want to spend happy hours in every garden center in the vicinity.

Then there are holidays. Quite a few Pigs felt they missed out last year and, even if they didn't, they feel they deserve something special in 2021. A long spa break somewhere glamorous could well be on the agenda.

Unfortunately, this is where your main glitches could occur, Pig. There's a 'but' in the generally positive tone of the year – there had to be, didn't there? Your 'but', Pig, involves the spending.

The Ox is incredibly tolerant of you, but the one thing Ox loathes is too much frivolous spending combined with a lack of dedication to work. Normally, this isn't too much of a problem as the Ox's affection for your charms allows you to indulge as much as you like.

This year, however, you're tempted to take things way too far. When two water signs get together, there's likely to be a flood of some kind, and for you – in 2021 – this flood appears to involve your cash flow – as in, there's plenty flowing in, but even more flowing out.

What's more, this is the one area where the Ox tends to lose patience if you overdo things even more than usual. So if you take reckless liberties with your credit card this year, Pig, the consequences could be very painful.

Wise Pigs who count to ten before splashing out, however, and who try to stick to a budget, can look forward to a happy 2021.

What it Means to Be a Pig

It takes quite a confident person in the West to announce 'I'm a Pig' to an assembled gathering without embarrassment. Imagine the comments! And if they should happen to be at an event where food is being served, they'd never hear the end of the jokes.

Yet, if you were in China and came out with such a remark, chances are you'd get a very favorable response. You'd certainly not be a figure of fun.

The Chinese zodiac Pig – sometimes known as the Boar – is regarded as a lucky sign. Since flesh and blood pigs tend to have very large litters of baby piglets, they're believed to be a symbol of prosperity and plenty.

And given the Chinese fondness for pork, anyone who owned a pig or two would have been fortunate indeed.

What's more, people born in any Year of the Pig tend to be genuinely amiable types – perhaps the most well-liked of all the 12 signs of the zodiac. Cheerful, friendly, and lacking in ego, they have no enemies. They can fit in anywhere. Nobody objects to a Pig.

Pigs just can't help being kind, sympathetic, and tolerant. Should someone let them down, Pigs will just shrug and insist it wasn't their fault. Pigs tend to get let down over and over again by the same people, but it never occurs to them to bear a grudge. They forgive and forget and move happily along. Friends may scold and warn them not to be a soft touch, but Pigs can't help it. They see no point in conflict.

That's not to say it's impossible to annoy a Pig, just that it takes a great deal to rouse the sweet Pig's nature to anger.

The other refreshing thing about the Pig is that they just want to be happy and have a good time – and they usually do. They find fun in the most unpromising situations, and their enthusiasm is infectious. Soon, everyone else is having fun too.

It's true Pigs enjoy their food – perhaps a little too much – but that's because they are a sensuous sign, appreciating physical pleasures; and it makes them very sexy too.

Shopping is a favorite hobby of many Pigs. They're not greedy; they just love spending money on pretty things simply for the sheer delight of discovering a new treasure and taking it home. This sometimes gets the Pig into trouble because finance isn't a strong point, but such is Pig's charm, they usually get away with it.

Pigs don't tend to be madly ambitious. They have no interest in the rat-race yet they are intelligent and conscientious and can't help being highly effective at work, despite having no ulterior motive or game plan. They often end up in managerial roles. Their sympathetic and conciliatory approach, coupled with their willingness to ask others for advice, goes down well in most organizations and usually leads to promotion. What's more, while avoiding unpleasantness wherever possible, the Pig doesn't like to give up on a task once started, and will invariably find a way to get it done that other signs wouldn't have thought of.

The Pig home reflects the sensuous nature of the Pig. Everything will be comfortable and warm with fabrics and furnishings that feel good as well as look good. Items will be chosen for ease of use rather than style, and there will probably be a great many objects and knick-knacks dotted around, picked up on Pig's shopping expeditions. Pigs quite often excel at cooking, and the Pig kitchen is likely to be crammed with all the latest gadgets and devices for food preparation.

Pigs approve of holidays, of course, and take as many as they can. They're not desperate to tackle extreme sports or go on dangerous expeditions, but they can be adventurous too. They like to be out in the open air, especially if it involves picnics and barbecues but, basically, easy-going Pig's just happy to take a break.

Best Jobs for Pig

Chef

5-star B&B owner

Party Planner

Aromatherapist

Chocolatier

Gift shop manager

HR consultant

Perfect Partners

Cupid's arrow can strike anywhere at any time, of course, but once the novelty of new romance wears off, some relationships are easier to maintain than others. Here's a guide to the Pig's compatibility with other signs.

Pig with Pig

When one Pig sets eyes on another Pig, they can't help moving closer for a better look, and should they get talking they probably won't stop. These two understand each other and share so many interests and points of view they seem like a perfect couple. Yet, long-term, they can end up feeling too alike. Pigs rarely argue, yet oddly enough they can find themselves squabbling over trivialities with another Pig. Care needed.

Pig with Rat

It's very easy for Rat to be beguiled by the Pig. Pig's easy-going, sympathetic nature immediately relaxes the Rat. What's more, Pig loves shopping as much as Rat so the two of them could enjoy many happy expeditions together. Conflict could occur through overspending. Pig does not understand Rat's compulsion to bag a bargain. Pig will buy whatever the price and the two could end up arguing over money.

Pig with Ox

Delightful Pig will catch Ox's eye, and since Pig isn't a constant thrill-seeker, the two of them could enjoy many peaceful evenings together, perhaps over a tasty meal. Yet Pig's spendthrift ways – at least in Ox's eyes – could soon prove very annoying as well as illogical to the Ox, while Pig could find Ox's attitude judgmental and upsetting. Not ideal for the long-term.

Pig with Tiger

Carefree Pig will love to bask in Tiger's impressive aura, while Tiger will feel good about protecting this charming but unworldly creature. They enjoy each other's company and Tiger, so focused on lofty matters, will find Pig's compulsive shopping too trivial to worry about. This couple could do well together as long as Pig's fondness for cozy nights in doesn't make Tiger feel trapped.

Pig with Rabbit

Pig is not quite as interested in fine dining as Rabbit, and is happy to scoff a burger as much as a cordon bleu creation, but their shared love of the good things in life makes these two happy companions. Once again, Pig's spending habits might irritate Rabbit, but not too much as Rabbit is quite willing to splurge on lovely things for the home. A relationship would work well.

Pig with Dragon

While Dragon and Pig might seem to be opposites, the two of them can create a surprisingly contented relationship. Pig is quite happy for Dragon to fly around doing exciting things as long as Pig is not expected to do much more than admire profusely. Dragon appreciates Pig's uncritical support and makes allowances for Pig's lack of stamina. This couple could live in harmony.

Pig with Snake

Pig and Snake don't have a lot to say to each other. Snake can't be bothered with Pig's endless shopping, and Pig is hurt by Snake's snobbish attitude. They both enjoy the good things in life so a luxury fling could briefly be fun – a shared spa break might be a good idea – but in the long-term, this relationship is probably not worth pursuing.

Pig with Horse

Pig and Horse are good companions. Horse is soothed by easy-going Pig and Pig is proud to be seen with such an alluring creature as Horse. They don't have a lot of interests in common, but they don't antagonize each other either. They can jog along amicably for quite a while, but long-term they may find they each want more than the other can provide.

Pig with Goat

Happy-go-lucky Pig and laid-back Goat make a good pair. They hate to stir up trouble and always look for a peaceful solution to any challenge. Ideally, they'd avoid the challenge altogether. They could be very contented together as long as Pig's spending and Goat's inability to deal with finances doesn't get them into trouble.

Pig with Monkey

On the surface, these two might seem an unlikely couple. Yet Pig enjoys Monkey's fun and humor while Monkey is happy to be admired uncritically. What's more, Monkey's inventive mind can solve any difficulties caused by Pig's spending, and since Monkey can't resist a challenge, the opportunity to retrain Pig or at least find a way to obtain purchases cheaper could help the relationship last.

Pig with Rooster

These two might seem an unlikely couple – modest Pig with extrovert Rooster. Yet Pig has no need or wish to crow, and can see the vulnerable character that lurks beneath Rooster's fine feathers. While Rooster responds to Pig's kindness and undemanding nature. As long as Rooster doesn't get bored, this can be a contented relationship.

Pig with Dog

In the outside world, the dog and the pig can get along well together; in fact, pigs, being intelligent creatures, can do many of the things dogs can do, so it's not surprising this zodiac pair make a good couple. Good-natured Pig is uncomplicated and fair-minded which suits Dog perfectly. Also, Pig brings out Dog's playful side – which delights Pig who's always keen to have a playmate. A happy relationship involving many restaurants.

Pig Love 2021 Style

You've always been a sexy sign, Pig, and popular too; so the Pig love life is seldom dull. This year, you could excel yourself. There's only so much Zoom trysting a single Pig can bear, and now solo Pigs are determined to get out there and enjoy some proper flesh and blood cuddles.

Finding willing playmates will not be a problem, and unattached Pigs can look forward to a year of delightful romance. Just make sure that new partners understand your freewheeling approach, Pig. At the moment, you're looking for fun and flirtation and the more the merrier, but things could turn awkward if you hook up with someone wanting to get serious.

The traditional Ox encourages couples to settle down, so quite a few misunderstandings could arise under this energy. A number of other signs are desperate to find a life partner this year and to them, you with your friendly, light-hearted personality could appear ideal. You may not see it that way, so tread carefully. Of course, it's not impossible that true love will wander into your orbit in 2021, but at the moment, many single Pigs could fail to notice. Towards the end of the year, though, you may suddenly realize a certain person has stayed the course, and it could be time to get exclusive.

Many attached Pigs, on the other hand, have rather enjoyed digging in with their partner during lockdown and creating cozy evenings 'a deux'. Yet, by now, even the two of you are eager to get out and – at the very least – put your trotters on the dance floor. Of course, some Pigs may have seen rather too much of their partners over the last 12 months, and this may be the moment to go your separate ways. If the relationship is strong, however, 2021 could see it getting stronger still.

Secrets of Success in 2021

Chances are that – this year – the typical Pig is not particularly interested in material success. After such a long spell of limiting most of the fun activities that bring Pigs so much joy, in 2021 many Pigs will be more interested in concentrating their energies on delightful entertainments. Earning a living and building a career can wait on the back burner for a while. Despite this, the Pig is a capable sign and when you can tear yourself away from socializing, you can quite easily do well at work.

It could be that you're inspired to change course completely and combine work with pleasure; such as indulging your love of beautiful things and shopping by seeking out choice items at car boot sales and auction rooms and selling them at a profit online). This could turn into a lucrative business for you, Pig, as long as you can bear to part with your finds once you've tracked them down.

And you won't lack for money. Cash will flow your way without you having to put in too much effort, thanks to the metal influence of the year; however, the strong water element when you and the Ox get together could cause difficulties. Water encourages your spending and extravagance, Pig, but it is also associated with emotion. You could find yourself getting over-emotional at times, and making unwise decisions based on impulsive whims. You're a sucker for a hard-luck story this year, Pig, which could cost you dear, or you may splash out recklessly on some luxury to celebrate success or to cheer you up if things go wrong. Either way, you could regret it.

Hang on to your wallet, and your heart, and success is yours, Pig.

The Pig Year at a Glance

January – Phew… you're ready and eager to get started on a much better year. Just the excuse you need for a party.

February – A new project has caught your eye. This could turn out to be just the solution you're looking for. Check it out.

March – A surprise windfall has got your name on it. It may not be quite as much as you first thought, though, so don't spend it before it arrives.

April – Colleagues or friends are going through a tricky time. Chocolate might help, or maybe just a sympathetic ear.

May – Work is going well, but you could be juggling two romances at the same time. Don't let your love life take up all your attention.

June – Things get fiery. You may have to make a choice. Or possibly look elsewhere altogether.

July – Unexpected bills may take you by surprise. Don't panic. Think things through calmly and make a plan.

August – Despite the budget, a sunshine holiday is calling your name. Go for it, Pig, but don't bring back a suitcase of souvenirs.

September – That back-to-school feeling is inspiring you to start something new. Explore the idea in more depth. It could be your future.

October – the Pig homestead could do with a makeover. Time to visit the DIY store.

November – You've started your Christmas shopping and there's no stopping you. No point in suggesting restraint. Just check your bank account on a regular basis.

December – Covid permitting, Santa's Grotto is round at yours and you're loving creating a festive atmosphere. You'll be eating the leftovers well into 2022, but who cares?!? Enjoy.

Lucky colors 2021: Purple, Silver, Orange

Lucky numbers 2021: 3, 6, 9

CHAPTER 13: THE RAT

Rat Years

5 February 1924 – 24 January 1925

24 January 1936 – 10 February 1937

10 February 1948 – 28 January 1949

28 January 1960 – 14 February 1961

15 February 1972 – 2 February 1973

2 February 1984 – 19 February 1985

19 February 1996 – 7 February 1997

7 February 2008 – 25 January 2009

25 January 2020 – 11 February 2021

Natural Element: Water

Will 2021 be a Golden year for Rats?

Well done, Rat! You've just completed the rigors of your ruling year, in which you also ushered in a whole new era. In turn, you seem to have emerged from this awesome task relatively unscathed.

And what a year you produced. Let's face it, it's probably safe to say that 2020 is a year that will remain etched in the memories of the whole world for decades to come – though, unfortunately, not in a good way.

Yet, of course, it's unfair to blame people born under the sign of the celestial Rat for the mayhem unleashed over the past 12 months. Lively Rat energy always acts as a necessary catalyst for change, and we had plenty of warning that this energy was going to be particularly dramatic in 2020.

It's quite likely, too, that when the dust settles and enough time has gone by, we will look back and see that the events of the past year forced badly needed changes and improvements to be put in place, from which we all went on to benefit. Let's hope so.

But that's far in the future. For now, Rat, you're probably looking forward to a bit of a break in 2021. Surprisingly, if you're typical of your sign, you're not as exhausted and burned out from your ruling responsibilities as people might expect. Born survivors, Rats can scurry through the most challenging and extreme conditions and stroll out the other side with little more than a singed whisker. So, chances are, you've coped well and will simply enjoy a short spell of calm before setting off on your next adventure.

The great thing is, it looks as if you'll get your wish in 2021. This is because the Rat and the Ox – who's taken over the baton as this year's ruler – get along pretty well together. Faithful Ox can be trusted to continue and expand the innovations put in place by the Rat, so there's no friction between them. In turn, Ox's slower, more considered pace gives the Rat a welcome chance to recuperate after 12 months of heavy-duty ratting.

If you're typical of your sign, Rat, you will sense a feeling of relaxation beginning to flow over you almost from the moment the New Year opens. It's as if you can take a big sigh of relief and settle back into a comfy, welcoming armchair. This won't suit you for very long of course, being a restless Rat, but at the beginning of 2021, it's exactly what you need.

Yet, *don't* be deceived by the slow start. The year of the Ox will bring most Rats a variety of splendid opportunities. Like the Ox, the Rat is a water creature, and when the two of you get together, there tends to be a flood. One thing leads to another very quickly and, before you know it, you could be overwhelmed if you're not very careful. This year it looks as if it's career opportunities that will pour your way, Rat.

This could seem unfair to other signs since your year was the cause of many lost opportunities for certain other creatures, but that's the way of the world, Rat. It's not your fault and – right now – you need to concentrate on working out how to choose between your many options. The worst thing you can do is try to accept them all.

Promotion beckons at work for employed Rats. Your ingenious way with shortcuts and saving money is greatly in demand right now, and many a boss will be begging you to use your unique skills to turn the business around. Self-employed Rats can look forward to an endless stream of enquiries, particularly from people who had never thought of becoming clients before. Everyone's looking for a clever, economical solution to an individual problem and you know just how to handle things. Once you've worked your magic they'll be clients forever.

Yet, strangely, despite the wealth of new offers coming your way, it seems there's something you started last year – or an idea that sprang into your mind – that will interest you more, Rat. Many Rats were forced to put an exciting project on hold in 2020 because of the difficult circumstances. Now, instead of exploring the fresh choices on offer, you're inspired to return to this unfinished challenge and begin again.

It could be to do with property or some sort of business plan but whatever it is, Rat, it could be your passport to fortune. Since this is an Ox year, of course you won't get away with cutting corners and failing to check the fine details, but as long as you follow the rules and resist bending them, you'll prosper.

Since this is also a metal year and metal traditionally is thought to nurture and support water, finances shouldn't be a problem. Cash boosts will arrive just when you need them, Rat, and you'll find a way to raise funds for whatever project takes your fancy.

Once again, though, you need to watch out for that flooding water effect and resist the urge to invest in anything risky or to take adventurous chances. A small gamble can escalate into something serious in the blink of an eye; so step back, Rat, and play it safe.

Many Rats could be thinking of upgrading the Rat residence in 2021. You've got big ideas and the cash is flowing in. Yet, somehow, you could find yourself so swept up in that exciting new venture you just haven't got time to pin down the perfect replacement home.

The Rat social life looks like being a little quieter than usual – due to the influence of the more introverted Ox. Oddly though, despite being the gregarious type, chances are this won't bother you at all. You'll be so enthralled with your new project, or new role at work, that you'll scarcely notice, and your colleagues will become much more important to you this year. In fact, most of the socializing that goes on in Rat circles will probably involve workmates who are rapidly morphing into good friends.

And although you're reluctant to tear yourself away from career building, it looks as if many Rats will be persuaded away on some sort of luxury holiday. All in all, this looks like being a pivotal year for you, Rat.

What it Means to Be a Rat

It doesn't sound so good does it, to call yourself a Rat? In fact, it may seem strange to start the astrological cycle with such a controversial creature as the unwelcome rodent. Here in the West, we haven't a good word to say about them. We talk of 'plagues' of rats; they 'infest' dirty, derelict places; they hang around dustbins.

They're associated with disease, rubbish, and sewers, and if a rat should be spied near our homes, we'd be straight on the phone to pest control. They make us shudder. Describe a person as 'a rat', and you're certainly not paying them a compliment.

Yet the Chinese view things differently. When they think of the zodiac Rat, they're thinking not of the flea-ridden rodent with the disconcerting long, hairless tail. They're imagining a certain energy, certain admirable qualities they associate with the creature. Rats, after all, are a very successful species. They are great survivors; they're quick, intelligent, tenacious, and they seem to thrive almost anywhere, under any conditions. All excellent qualities to be commended, if you found them in a human.

So, far from being an unfortunate sign, being born in the year of the Rat is regarded as a good omen.

Rats possess great charm and elegance. They're chatty, intelligent, and make friends easily. At parties, people seem drawn to them. There's something about their genuine enjoyment of being surrounded by new faces that makes them easy to get along with. Yet, they value old friends too, will make an effort to stay in touch, and a friendship with a rat is likely to last a lifetime.

Both male and female rats always look good. They believe that outward appearances are important. Instinctively, they understand that you only get one chance to make a first impression, so they take care never to be caught off-guard looking a mess.

This happy knack is easier for them than most because they love shopping and are Olympic-standard bargain hunters. They can't resist a sale and if it's a designer outlet, so much the better. Their homes are usually equally smart for the same reason. Rats have innate good taste and are as thrilled with finding a stylish chair, or piece of artwork at half price, as they are a pair of shoes.

They enjoy spending money and the challenge of hunting down the best deal; and because they're also successful at work, they tend to have plenty of cash to splurge. Yet, despite this, Rats can often be viewed as a bit stingy. They're not mean, it's just that Rats' strong survival instincts lead them to prioritize themselves and their family when it comes to allocating their resources. Within their families, Rats are extremely generous.

Rats also enjoy the finer things in life. They prefer not to get their hands dirty if at all possible and are experts at getting other people to do mundane tasks for them. They like pampering and luxury and lavish holidays. Yet, being supremely adaptable, they will happily embark on a backpacking trip if it takes them where they want to go and there's no other option. They're adventurous, and hate to be bored, so they're prepared to take a calculated risk if some place or person catches their eye.

Yet, this willingness to take a risk combined with the love of a bargain can occasionally get them into trouble, despite their super-sensitive survival instincts. Rats, particularly male Rats, have to guard against the urge to gamble. The combination of the prospect of winning easy money, the excitement of the element of chance, and the challenge of pitting their wits against the odds can prove irresistible. What starts as a mild flirtation for fun can end up as quite a problem.

The same could be said for suspect 'get-rich-quick' schemes. Though clever and skeptical enough to see through them, Rats are so thrilled by the idea of an easy gain, the temptation to cast doubts aside, against their better judgement, can be overwhelming.

But if any sign can get away with such unwise habits, it's probably the Rat. Rats are good at making money and handling money. They're also masters at spotting an escape route and scuttling away down it if the going gets too tough. Underneath that gregarious bonhomie, there's a shrewd, observant brain that misses nothing. Rats have very sharp eyes and are highly observant even when they don't appear to be taking any notice. They are also very ambitious, though they tend to keep it quiet. Dazzled by their genuine charm and witty conversation, people often fail to see that most moves Rats make are taking them methodically to the top. It's no accident they call it 'the rat race'.

Best Jobs for Rats in 2021

Auctioneer

Financial Consultant

Property Developer

Sales Manager

Fashion Buyer

Wedding Planner

Media Consultant

Market Trader

Perfect Partners 2021

Cupid's arrow can strike anywhere at any time, of course, but once the novelty of new romance wears off, some relationships are easier to maintain than others. Here's a guide to the Rat's compatibility with other signs.

Rat with Rat

These two are certainly on the same wavelength and share many interests. When their eyes first meet, passionate sparks may fly. This relationship could work very well, though over time the competitive and ambitious nature of both partners could see them pulling in different directions. What's more, if one should succumb to a weakness for gambling or risky business ventures while the other does not, it will end in tears.

Rat with Ox

Oddly enough, this combination can be surprisingly successful. Frenetic Rat and calm Ox may seem to be opposites but, in fact, Rat can find Ox's laid-back approach strangely soothing. Ox is not interested in competing with Rat and will put up with Rat's scurrying after new schemes with patience. As long as Rat doesn't get bored and has enough excitement in other areas of life, this relationship could be very contented.

Rat with Tiger

The magnificent Tiger will always catch Rat's eye because Rat loves beautiful things, but Tiger's natural element is fire and Rat's is water and fire and water don't mix well. Tiger's not interested in Rat's latest bargain, and Rat doesn't share Tiger's passion for changing the world, yet the attraction is strong. If Rat makes an effort to step back and not get in Tiger's way, they could reach a good understanding.

Rat with Rabbit

Rat finds Rabbit intriguing. Here is an attractive, stylish creature that doesn't feel the need to be pushy or take center stage yet somehow manages to be at the heart of things. The Rat wants to find out more, while Rabbit is flattered and entertained by witty Rat's attention. These two respect each other but, over the long-term, Rat could be too overpowering.

Rat with Dragon

This couple is usually regarded as a very good match. They have much in common being action-loving, excitement-seeking personalities who hate to be bored. It takes a lot to dazzle Rat, but the Dragon's glamorous aura proves irresistible, while Dragon loves to be admired, so each enjoys being with the other. There could be the odd power struggle as these two are both strong characters, but the magnetism is so powerful they usually kiss and make up.

Rat with Snake

The Snake shares Rat's good taste and being elegant, sophisticated, and smart will delight Rat at first sight. These two get on very well on an intellectual level but perhaps are better as good friends rather than long-term partners. The Snake's love of basking in the sun for hours strikes Rat as lazy and dull, while Rat's need to rush around doing deals and meeting people seems pointless and wearying to the Snake.

Rat with Horse

Rat and Horse both fizz with energy and they love action and looking good, yet this is not seen as an ideal partnership. Nothing's impossible, of course, but these two will have to work hard to find harmony. The Rat will admire Horse's enthusiasm and cheerful approach but become impatient to discover Horse can also be fiery and emotional. Horse, on the other hand, can find Rat's risk-taking behavior extremely worrying.

Rat with Goat

The Rat is charmed by carefree Goat and fascinated by its artistic talent and happy knack of living in the present. Easy-going Goat tends to like everyone so is perfectly content to enjoy Rat's company. These two can get along fine, yet they don't really understand each other deep down. Long-term, the Rat may find Goat's lack of interest in the practical side of life, such as finances and bills, irritating.

Rat with Monkey

Unlikely as it might appear, mischievous Monkey and the clever Rat make a good partnership. Their quick minds, sociable natures, and love of novelty ensure that they're never bored together. True, Rat might sometimes feel Monkey is too inclined to skim over the surface of things and could do with being more serious at times, but Monkey's ingenuity and audaciousness always save the day. Both can have a weakness for gambling though, so need to take care.

Rat with Rooster

The first thing Rat notices about the Rooster is its beautiful plumage, but this a relationship which is unlikely to get much further than initial admiration. Rooster's direct and frank approach can strike the Rat as tactless, while the Rooster can't understand why Rat has to make life so convoluted and complicated. Then again, Rooster's natural confidence and aplomb can come across as bragging to the Rat. These two have to be very determined to make a partnership work.

Rat with Dog

The Rat and the Dog get along pretty well together. Both are strong characters, and they respect each other and give each other space when required. But deep down, the Dog is a worrier and gets anxious about unnecessary risks, while Rat just can't help sailing close to the wind if an interesting opportunity presents itself. Long-term, reckless Rat might unintentionally drive Dog to distraction. Only to be considered by Dogs with nerves of steel.

Rat with Pig

It's very easy for Rat to be beguiled by the Pig. Pig's easy-going, sympathetic nature immediately relaxes the Rat. What's more, Pig loves shopping as much as Rat so the two of them could enjoy many happy expeditions together. Conflict could occur through overspending. Pig does not understand Rat's compulsion to bag a bargain. Pig will buy at whatever the price and the two could Love

Rat Love 2021 Style

If you're typical of your sign, Rat, you love a party. You also love get-togethers, receptions, pub crawls, and any other excuse to mix with a crowd. In fact, single or spoken for, the Rat is popular everywhere, and you're never short of interested admirers.

Yet, this year is a little different. Single or partnered, many Rats will be so busy with their career that socializing is going to happen after hours when it looks as if the whole lot of you will just move from the workplace to the nearest bar or restaurant for a riotous evening. Suddenly, amidst the fun, single Rats could find themselves eyeing up a colleague and noticing for the first time how fit they are.

It might be frowned upon, it might even be against the rules, but an office romance could easily develop for single Rats this year. And maybe not just single Rats; attached Rats will have to tread carefully if they want their long term relationship at home to survive.

The great thing about office romances is that you both have such a lot in common and you already get on well. The 'less great' thing about them is that if things go wrong, it can all get horribly complicated at work. Not that such thoughts have ever bothered the reckless Rat unduly. The typical Rat enjoys it while it lasts and worries about the consequences when they happen. And being such a brilliant survivor, whichever way things turn out, chances are, you'll be just fine.

Attached Rats could find 2021 more tricky unless their relationship is exceptionally strong. Even if you manage not to succumb to temptation at work, Rat, there's a danger your partner will feel neglected and bored because you're hardly ever around. If you want to keep the romance alive, timetable some date nights in your diary and make sure you keep them!

Secret of Success in 2021

You're onto something big this year, Rat. Plans that had to be shelved due to the upheavals of 2020 are now coming back on-stream along with new offers and opportunities. You've got so much choice, you could get dizzy. The only problem is in deciding which direction to take.

This fortunate outlook is down to the supportive metal element of the year, which aims to nurture your efforts and also provide the finances to help them expand. It combines with the benevolent attitude of the Ox, which will ensure that helpful people cross your path just when you need them most. All you have to do is keep your head down, work diligently, and refrain from messing things up! So, how could you mess things up? Quite easily if you indulge in too much Rat-like behavior. You don't do dull, Rat, so plodding along in the same old way for too long bores you. You prefer to work at speed and then dash off to the next challenge. The Ox, though, demands patience, stamina, and a thorough approach. Resist the urge to skip to the end of a task and bolt. Check and recheck, and the Ox will reward your efforts.

Most of all, regard all golden opportunities, 'can't fail' schemes, and 'sure-fire winners', with your most skeptical eye. You are a highly intelligent creature, Rat, but your eagerness to find a fast track to success, and also to believe there is such a thing often leads you to delude yourself. As the Ox would probably say, there's no substitute for sheer hard work. Follow that advice, and you really can't fail this year.

The Rat Year at a Glance

January – Are things really this slow and quiet? Don't knock it. Relax and ease yourself into the Ox year.

February – Your energy is rising, and you can feel the pace beginning to quicken. A brilliant idea inspires you.

March – You're keen to get going on an exciting project. An authority figure approves, and you're on your way.

April – An extroverted, influential figure crosses your path. They point the way to success. Take their advice.

May – Now's the time to settle in and get some hard work completed. Your efforts will get you noticed.

June – A flirty person catches your eye. You're tempted to escape your responsibilities and have some fun. Oh, go on then!

July – That project is calling again, but social stars are blazing. Time to juggle. You can have your cake and eat it if you're clever.

August – Someone in your circle is talking holidays. You really don't have time but all work and no play as they say… Looks like you'll find the time for a break.

September – Work is piling up again, and an annoying colleague interferes. Don't lose your temper Rat – you're good at diplomacy; make an effort.

October – Someone on the social scene is getting emotional. You don't like dramas, but you can calm this down.

November – Rewards are heading your way. Whatever you're up to will profit and thrive.

December – This is actually your month, Rat, and everything's going your way. Think Christmas bonus or unexpected windfall and some fabulous parties to celebrate.

Lucky colors for 2021: Emerald, Purple and White

Lucky numbers for 2021: 1, 5

CHAPTER 14: BUT THEN THERE'S SO MUCH MORE TO YOU

So now you know your animal sign, but possibly you're thinking – okay, but how can everyone born in the same year as me have the same personality as me?

You've only got to think back to your class at school, full of children the same age as you, to know this can't be true. And you're absolutely right. What's more, Chinese astrologers agree with you. For this reason, in Chinese astrology, your birth year is only the beginning. The month you were born and the hour of your birth are also ruled by the twelve zodiac animals – and not necessarily the same animal that rules your birth year.

These other animals then go on to modify the qualities of your basic year personality. So someone born in an extrovert Tiger year but at the time of day ruled by the quieter Ox, and in the month of the softly spoken Snake, for instance, would very likely find their risk-taking Tiger qualities much toned down and enhanced by a few other calmer, more subtle traits.

By combining these three important influences, you get a much more accurate and detailed picture of the complex and unique person you really are. These calculations lead to so many permutations it soon becomes clear how people born in the same year can share various similarities, yet still remain quite different from each other.

What's more, the other animals linked to your date of birth can also have a bearing on how successful you will be in any year and how well you get on with people from other signs. Traditionally, the Horse and the Rabbit don't get on well together, for instance, so you'd expect two people born in these years to be unlikely to end up good friends. Yet if both individuals had other compatible signs in their charts, they could find themselves surprisingly warming to each other.

This is how it works:

Your Outer Animal – (Birth Year | Creates Your First Impression)

You're probably completely unaware of it, but when people meet you for the first time, they will sense the qualities represented by the animal that ruled your birth year. Your Outer Animal and its personality influence the way you appear to the outside world. Your Outer animal is your public face. You may not feel the least bit like this creature deep down, and you may wonder why nobody seems to understand the real you. Why is it that people always seem to underestimate you, or perhaps overestimate you, you may ask yourself frequently. The reason is that you just can't help giving the impression of your birth-year animal and people will tend to see you and think of you in this way – especially if they themselves were born in other years.

Your Inner Animal – (Birth Month I The Private You)

Your Inner Animal is the animal that rules the month in which you were born. The personality of this creature tells you a lot about how you feel inside, what motivates you, and how you tend to live your life. When you're out in the world and want to present yourself in the best light, it's easy for you to project the finest talents of your birth-year animal. You've got them at your fingertips. But at home, with no one you need to impress, your Inner Animal comes to the fore. You can kick back and relax. You may find you have abilities and interests that no one at work would ever guess. Only your closest friends and loved ones are likely to get to know your Inner Animal.

By now you know your Outer Animal so you can move on to find your Inner Animal from the chart below:

Month of Birth - Your Inner Animal

January – the Ox

February – the Tiger

March – the Rabbit

April – the Dragon

May – the Snake

June – the Horse

July – the Goat

August – the Monkey

September – the Rooster

October – the Dog

November – the Pig

December – the Rat

Your Secret Animal – (Birth Hour | The Still, Small Voice Within)

Your secret animal rules the time you were born. Each 24-hour period is divided into 12, two-hour time-slots and each slot is believed to be ruled by a particular animal. This animal represents the deepest, most secret part of you. It's possibly the most intimate, individual part of you as it marks the moment you first entered the world and became 'you'. This animal is possibly your conscience and your inspiration. It might represent qualities you'd like to have or sometimes fail to live up to. Chances are, no one else will ever meet your Secret Animal.

For your Secret Animal check out the time of your birth:

Hours of Birth – Your Secret Animal

1 am – 3 am – the Ox

3 am – 5 am – the Tiger

5 am – 7 am – the Rabbit

7 am – 9 am – the Dragon

9 am – 11 am – the Snake

11 am – 1.00 pm – the Horse

1.00 pm – 3.00 pm – the Goat

3.00 pm – 5.00 pm – the Monkey

5.00 pm – 7.00 pm – the Rooster

7.00 pm – 9.00 pm – the Dog

9.00 pm – 11.00 pm – the Pig

11.00 pm – 1.00 am – the Rat

When you've found your other animals, go back to the previous chapters and read the sections on those particular signs. You may well discover talents and traits that you recognise immediately as belonging to you in addition to those mentioned in your birth year. It could also be that your Inner Animal or your Secret Animal is the same as your Year animal. A Dragon born at 8 am in the morning, for instance, will be a secret Dragon inside as well as outside, because the hours between 7 am and 9 am are ruled by the Dragon.

When this happens, it suggests that the positive and the less positive attributes of the Dragon will be held in harmony, so this particular Dragon ends up being very well balanced.

You might also like to look at your new animal's compatibility with other signs and see where you might be able to widen your circle of friends and improve your love life.

CHAPTER 15: IN YOUR ELEMENT

There's no doubt about it, Chinese astrology has many layers. But then we all recognize that we have many facets to our personalities, too. We are all more complicated than we might first appear. And more unique, as well.

It turns out that even people who share the same Birth Year sign are not identical to people with the same sign but born in different years. A Rabbit born in 1963, for instance, will express their Rabbit personality in a slightly different way to a Rabbit born in 1975. This is not simply down to the influence of the other animals in their chart, it's because each year is also believed to be ruled by one of the five Chinese 'elements', as well as the year animal.

These elements are known as Water, Wood, Fire, Earth, and Metal.

Each element is thought to contain special qualities which are bestowed onto people born in the year it ruled, in addition to the qualities of their animal sign.

Since there are 12 signs endlessly rotating, and five elements, the same animal and element pairing only recurs once every 60 years. Which is why babies born in this 2021 year of the Golden Ox are unlikely to grow up remembering much about other Metal Oxen from the previous generation. Those senior Oxen will already be 60-years-old when the new calves are born.

In years gone by, when life expectancy was much lower, the chances are there would only ever be one generation of a particular combined sign and element alive in the world at a time.

Find Your Element from the Chart Below:

The 1920s

5 February 1924 – 24 January 1925 | RAT | WOOD

25 January 1925 – 12 February 1926 | OX | WOOD

13 February 1926 – 1 February 1927 | TIGER | FIRE

2 February 1927 – 22 January 1928 | RABBIT | FIRE

23 January 1928 – 9 February 1929 | DRAGON | EARTH

10 February 1929 – 29 January 1930 | SNAKE | EARTH

The 1930s

30 January 1930 – 16 February 1931 | HORSE | METAL

17 February 1931 – 5 February 1932 | GOAT | METAL

6 February 1932 – 25 January 1933 | MONKEY | WATER

26 January 1933 – 13 February 1934 | ROOSTER | WATER

14 February 1934 – 3 February 1935 | DOG | WOOD

4 February 1935 – 23 January 1936 | PIG | WOOD

24 January 1936 – 10 February 1937 | RAT | FIRE

11 February 1937 – 30 January 1938 | OX | FIRE

31 January 1938 – 18 February 1939 | TIGER | EARTH

19 February 1939 – 7 February 1940 | RABBIT | EARTH

The 1940s

8 February 1940 – 26 January 1941 | DRAGON | METAL

27 January 1941 – 14 February 1942 | SNAKE | METAL

15 February 1942 – 4 February 1943 | HORSE | WATER

5 February 1943 – 24 January 1944 | GOAT | WATER

25 January 1944 – 12 February 1945 | MONKEY | WOOD

13 February 1945 – 1 February 1946 | ROOSTER | WOOD

2 February 1946 – 21 January 1947 | DOG | FIRE

22 January 1947 – 9 February 1948 | PIG | FIRE

10 February 1948 – 28 January 1949 | RAT | EARTH

29 January 1949 – 16 February 1950 | OX | EARTH

The 1950s

17 February 1950 – 5 February 1951 | TIGER | METAL

6 February 1951 – 26 January 1952 | RABBIT | METAL

27 January 1952 – 13 February 1953 | DRAGON | WATER

14 February 1953 – 2 February 1954 | SNAKE | WATER

3 February 1954 – 23 January 1955 | HORSE | WOOD

24 January 1955 – 11 February 1956 | GOAT | WOOD

12 February 1956 – 30 January 1957 | MONKEY | FIRE

31 January 1957 – 17 February 1958 | ROOSTER | FIRE

18 February 1958 – 7 February 1959 | DOG | EARTH

8 February 1959 – 27 January 1960 | PIG | EARTH

The 1960s

28 January 1960 – 14 February 1961 | RAT | METAL

15 February 1961 – 4 February 1962 | OX | METAL

5 February 1962 – 24 January 1963 | TIGER | WATER

25 January 1963 – 12 February 1964 | RABBIT | WATER

13 February 1964 – 1 February 1965 | DRAGON | WOOD

2 February 1965 – 20 January 1966 | SNAKE | WOOD

21 January 1966 – 8 February 1967 | HORSE | FIRE

9 February 1967 – 29 January 1968 | GOAT | FIRE

30 January 1968 – 16 February 1969 | MONKEY | EARTH

17 February 1969 – 5 February 1970 | ROOSTER | EARTH

The 1970s

6 February 1970 – 26 January 1971 | DOG | METAL

27 January 1971 – 14 February 1972 | PIG | METAL

15 February 1972 – 2 February 1973 | RAT | WATER

3 February 1973 – 22 January 1974 | OX | WATER

23 January 1974 – 10 February 1975 | TIGER | WOOD

11 February 1975 – 30 January 1976 | RABBIT | WOOD

31 January 1976 – 17 February 1977 | DRAGON | FIRE

18 February 1977 – 6 February 1978 | SNAKE | FIRE

7 February 1978 – 27 January 1979 | HORSE | EARTH

28 January 1979 – 15 February 1980 | GOAT | EARTH

The 1980s

16 February 1980 – 4 February 1981 | MONKEY | METAL

5 February 1981 – 24 January 1982 | ROOSTER | METAL

25 January 1982 – 12 February 1983 | DOG | WATER

13 February 1983 – 1 February 1984 | PIG | WATER

2 February 1984 – 19 February 1985 | RAT | WOOD

20 February 1985 – 8 February 1986 | OX | WOOD

9 February 1986 – 28 January 1987 | TIGER | FIRE

29 January 1987 – 16 February 1988 | RABBIT | FIRE

17 February 1988 – 5 February 1989 | DRAGON | EARTH

6 February 1989 – 26 January 1990 | SNAKE | EARTH

The 1990s

27 January 1990 – 14 February 1991 | HORSE | METAL

15 February 1991 – 3 February 1992 | GOAT | METAL

4 February 1992 – 22 January 1993 | MONKEY | WATER

23 January 1993 – 9 February 1994 | ROOSTER | WATER

10 February 1994 – 30 January 1995 | DOG | WOOD

31 January 1995 – 18 February 1996 | PIG | WOOD

19 February 1996 – 7 February 1997 | RAT | FIRE

8 February 1997 – 27 January 1998 | OX | FIRE

28 January 1998 – 5 February 1999 | TIGER | EARTH

6 February 1999 – 4 February 2000 | RABBIT | EARTH

The 2000s

5 February 2000 – 23 January 2001 | DRAGON | METAL

24 January 2001 – 11 February 2002 | SNAKE | METAL

12 February 2002 – 31 January 2003 | HORSE | WATER

1 February 2003 – 21 January 2004 | GOAT | WATER

22 January 2004 – 8 February 2005 | MONKEY | WOOD

9 February 2005 – 28 January 2006 | ROOSTER | WOOD

29 January 2006 – 17 February 2007 | DOG | FIRE

18 February 2007 – 6 February 2008 | PIG | FIRE

7 February 2008 – 25 January 2009 | RAT | EARTH

26 January 2009 – 13 February 2010 | OX | EARTH

The 2010s

14 February 2010 – 2 February 2011 | TIGER | METAL

3 February 2011 – 22 January 2012 | RABBIT | METAL

23 January 2012 – 9 February 2013 | DRAGON | WATER

10 February 2013 – 30 January 2014 | SNAKE | WATER

31 January 2014 – 18 February 2015 | HORSE | WOOD

19 February 2015 – 7 February 2016 | GOAT | WOOD

8 February 2016 – 27 January 2017 | MONKEY | FIRE

28 January 2017 – 15 February 2018 | ROOSTER | FIRE

16 February 2018 – 4 February 2019 | DOG | EARTH

5 February 2019 – 24 January 2020 | PIG | EARTH

The 2020s

25 January 2020 – 11 February 2021 | RAT | METAL

12 February 2021 – 1 February 2022 | OX | METAL

2 February 2022 – 21 January 2023 | TIGER | WATER

22 January 2023 – 9 February 2024 | RABBIT | WATER

10 February 2024 – 28 January 2025 | DRAGON | WOOD

29 January 2025 – 16 February 2026 | SNAKE | WOOD

17 February 2026 – 5 February 2027 | HORSE | FIRE

6 February 2027 – 25 January 2028 | GOAT | FIRE

26 January 2028 – 12 February 2029 | MONKEY | EARTH

13 February 2029 – 2 February 2030 | ROOSTER | EARTH

You may have noticed that the 'natural' basic element of your sign is not necessarily the same as the element of the year you were born. Don't worry about this. The element of your birth year takes precedence, though you could also read the qualities assigned to the natural element as well, as these will be relevant to your personality but to a lesser degree.

Metal

Metal is the element associated in China with gold and wealth. So if you are a Metal child, you will be very good at accumulating money. The Metal individual is ambitious, even if their animal sign is not particularly career-minded. The Metal-born version of an unworldly sign will still somehow have an eye for a bargain or a good investment; they'll manage to buy at the right time when prices are low and be moved to sell just as the price is peaking. If they want to get rid of unwanted items, they'll potter along to a car boot sale and without appearing to try, somehow make a killing, selling the lot while stalls around them struggle for attention. Career-minded signs with the element Metal have to be careful they don't overdo things. They have a tendency to become workaholics. Wealth will certainly flow, but it could be at the expense of family harmony and social life.

The element of Metal adds power, drive, and tenacity to whatever sign it influences so if you were born in a Metal year you'll never lack cash for long.

Water

Water is the element associated with communication, creativity, and the emotions. Water has a knack of flowing around obstacles, finding routes that are not obvious to the naked eye and seeping into the smallest cracks. So if you're a Water child, you'll be very good at getting what you want in an oblique, unchallenging way. You are one of nature's lateral thinkers. You are also wonderful with people. You're sympathetic, empathetic, and can always find the right words at the right time. You can also be highly persuasive, but in such a subtle way nobody notices your influence or input. They think the whole thing was their own idea.

People born in Water years are very creative and extremely intuitive. They don't know where their inspiration comes from, but somehow ideas just pour into their brains. Many artists were born in Water years.

Animal signs that are normally regarded as a little impatient and tactless have their rough edges smoothed when they appear in a Water year. People born in these years will be more diplomatic, artistic, and amiable than other versions of their fellow signs. And if you were born in a naturally sensitive, emotional sign, in a Water year, you'll be so intuitive you're probably psychic. Yet just as water can fall as gentle nurturing rain, or a raging destructive flood, so Water types need to take care not to let their emotions run away with them or to allow themselves to use their persuasive skills to be too manipulative.

Wood

Wood is the element associated with growth and expansion. In Chinese astrology, Wood doesn't primarily refer to the inert variety used to make floorboards and furniture, it represents living, flourishing trees and smaller plants, all pushing out of the earth and growing towards the sky.

Wood is represented by the colour green, not brown. If you're a Wood child, you're likely to be honest, generous, and friendly. You think BIG and like to be involved in numerous projects, often at the same time.

Wood people are practical yet imaginative and able to enlist the support of others simply by the sincerity and enthusiasm with which they tackle their plans. Yet even though they're always busy with a project, they somehow radiate calm, stability, and confidence. There's a sense of the timeless serenity of a big old tree about Wood people. Other signs instinctively trust them and look to them for guidance.

Animal signs that could be prone to nervousness or impulsive behaviour tend to be calmer and more productive in Wood year versions, while signs whose natural element is also Wood could well end up leaders of vast teams or business empires. Wood people tend to sail smoothly through life, but they must guard against becoming either stubborn or unyielding as they grow older or alternatively, saying 'yes' to every new plan and overextending themselves.

Fire

Fire is the element associated with dynamism, strength, and persistence. Fire demands action, movement, and expansion. It also creates a huge amount of heat. Fire is precious when it warms our homes and cooks our food, and it possesses a savage beauty that's endlessly fascinating. Yet it's also highly dangerous and destructive if it gets out of control. Something of this ambivalent quality is evident in Fire children.

People born in Fire years tend to be immensely attractive, magnetic types. Other signs are drawn to them. Yet there is always a hint of danger, of unpredictability, about them. You never know quite where you are with a Fire year sign and in a way, this is part of their fascination.

People born in Fire years like to get things done. They are extroverted and bold and impatient for action. They are brilliant at getting things started and energising people and projects. Quieter signs born in a Fire year are more dynamic, outspoken, and energetic than their fellow sign cousins, while extrovert signs positively blaze with exuberance and confidence when Fire is added to the mix.

People born in Fire years will always be noticed, but they should try to remember they tend to be impatient and impulsive. Develop a habit of pausing to take a deep breath to consider things, before rushing in, and you won't get burned.

Earth

Earth is the element associated with patience, stability, and practicality. This may not sound exciting but, in Chinese astrology, Earth is at the centre of everything: the heart of the planet. Earth year children are strong, hardworking personalities. They will persist with a task if it's worthwhile and never give up until it's complete. They create structure and balance, and they have very nurturing instincts.

Women born in Earth years make wonderful mothers, and if they're not mothering actual children, they'll be mothering their colleagues at work, or their friends and relatives, while also filling their homes with houseplants and raising vegetables in the garden if at all possible.

Other signs like being around Earth types as they exude a sense of security. Earth people don't like change, and they strive to keep their lives settled and harmonious. They are deeply kind and caring and immensely honest. Tact is not one of their strong points, however. They will always say what they think, so if you don't want the unvarnished truth, better not to ask!

Earth lends patience and stability to the more flighty, over-emotional signs, and rock solid integrity to the others. Earth people will be sought-after in whatever field they choose to enter, but they must take care not to become too stubborn. Make a point of seeking out and listening to a wide range of varying opinions before setting a decision in stone.

Yin and Yang

As you looked down the table of years and elements, you may have noticed that the elements came in pairs. Each element was repeated the following year. If the Monkey was Water one year, it would be followed immediately the next year by the Rooster, also Water.

This is because of Yin and Yang – the mysterious but vital forces that, in Chinese philosophy, are believed to control the planet and probably the whole universe. They can be thought of as positive and negative, light and dark, masculine and feminine, night and day, etc. but the important point is that everything is either Yin or Yang; the two forces complement each other and both are equally important because only together do they make up the whole. For peace and harmony to be achieved, both forces need to be in balance.

Each of the animal signs is believed to be either Yin or Yang and because of the need for balance and harmony, they alternate through the years. Six of the 12 signs are Yin and six are Yang and since Yang represents extrovert, dominant energy, the Yang sign is first, followed by the Yin sign which represents quiet, passive force. A Yang sign is always followed by a Yin sign throughout the cycle.

The Yang signs are:

Rat

Tiger

Dragon

Horse

Monkey

Dog

The Yin Signs are

Ox

Rabbit

Snake

Goat

Rooster

Pig

Although Yang is seen as a masculine energy, and Yin a feminine energy, in reality, whether you are male or female, everyone has a mixture of Yin and Yang within them. If you need to know, quickly, whether your sign is Yin or Yang just check your birth year. If it ends in an even number (or 0) your sign is Yang. If it ends in an odd number, your sign is Yin.

In general, Yang signs tend to be extrovert, action-oriented types while Yin signs are gentler, more thoughtful, and patient.

So, as balance is essential when an element controls a period of time, it needs to express itself in its stronger Yang form in a Yang year as well as in its gentler Yin form in a Yin year, to be complete.

That's why this year of the Metal Ox (Yin) completes the Metal element which began last year with the Yang Rat and the stage is set for Water in 2022.

But why do elements have two forms? It's to take into account the great variations in strength encompassed by an element. The difference between a candle flame and a raging inferno – both belonging to Fire; or a great oak tree and a little seedling – both belonging to the Wood element.

In Yang years, the influence of the ruling element will be particularly strong. In Yin years, the same element expresses itself in its gentler form.

Friendly Elements

Just as some signs get on well together and others don't, so some elements work well together while others don't. These are the elements that exist in harmony:

METAL likes EARTH and WATER

WATER likes METAL and WOOD

WOOD likes WATER and FIRE

FIRE likes WOOD and EARTH

EARTH likes FIRE and METAL

The reason for these friendly partnerships is believed to be the natural, productive cycle. Water nourishes Wood and makes plants grow, Wood provides fuel for Fire, Fire produces ash which is a type of Earth, Earth can be melted or mined to produce Metal while Metal contains or carries Water in a bucket.

So, Water supports Wood, Wood supports Fire, Fire supports Earth, Earth supports Metal and Metal supports Water.

Unfriendly Elements

But since everything has to be in balance, all the friendly elements are opposed by the same number of unfriendly elements. These are the elements that are not in harmony:

METAL dislikes WOOD and FIRE

WATER dislikes FIRE and EARTH

WOOD dislikes EARTH and METAL

FIRE dislikes METAL and WATER

EARTH dislikes WOOD and WATER

The reason some elements don't get on is down to the destructive cycle which is: Water puts out Fire and is absorbed by Earth, Wood breaks up Earth (with its strong roots) and is harmed by Metal tools, Metal is melted by fire and can cut down Wood.

So if someone just seems to rub you up the wrong way, for no logical reason, it could be that your elements clash.

CHAPTER 16: WESTERN HOROSCOPES AND CHINESE HOROSCOPES – THE LINK

So now, hopefully, you'll have all the tools you need to create your very own, personal, multi-faceted Chinese horoscope. But does that mean your more familiar Western-style astrological sign is no longer relevant?

Not necessarily. Purists may not agree, but the odd thing is there does seem to be an overlap between a person's Western birth sign and their Chinese birth month sign; the two together can add yet another interesting layer to the basic birth year personality.

A Rabbit born under the Western sign of Leo may turn out to be very different on the surface, to a Rabbit born under the Western sign of Pisces for instance.

Of course, Chinese astrology already takes this into account by including the season of birth in a full chart, but we can possibly refine the system even further by adding the characteristics we've learned from our Western Sun Signs into the jigsaw.

If you'd like to put this theory to the test, simply find your Chinese year sign and then look up your Western Astrological sign within it, from the list below. While you're at it, why not check out the readings for your partner and friends too? You could be amazed at how accurate the results turn out to be.

Ox

Aries Ox

Dynamic Aries brings the Ox a very welcome blast of fire and urgency to stir those methodical bones into faster action. This is a fortunate combination because when the steadfast, industrious, patient qualities of the Ox are combined with quickness of mind and a definite purpose, very little can stand in the way of this subject's progress. Aries Oxen do particularly well in careers where enormous discipline combined with flair and intelligence is required. Many writers are born under this sign as are college lecturers, historical researchers and archaeologists.

Taurus Ox

Oxen are notoriously stubborn creatures but combine them with Taurus the bull and this trait is doubled if not quadrupled. It is not a good idea to box these types into a corner because they will take a stand and refuse to budge even if the house is on fire. Taurean Oxen really will cut off their noses to spite their faces if they feel they have to. Fall out with them and stop talking, and the chances are that the feud will continue to the grave. Yet despite this tendency, Oxen born under the sign of Taurus are not unfriendly types. They are utterly reliable and totally loyal. Family and friends trust them completely. They might be a bit old fashioned and inflexible, but they are lovable too.

Gemini Ox

Chatty Gemini transforms the normally taciturn Ox into a beast which is almost loquacious, at least by the normal standards of these strong silent types. They might even be confident enough to attempt a few jokes, and though humor is not the Oxen's strongpoint, the Gemini Ox can usually produce something respectably amusing if not sidesplittingly funny. Oddly enough, should the Ox set his mind to it and apply his awesome hard work and patience to the subject of humor he might even make a career of it. Some Gemini Oxen have even become accomplished comedians – not simply through natural talent but through sheer hard work and perseverance. More frequently, however, the combination of Gemini with the Ox produces a 'poor man's lawyer' – a highly opinionated individual who can see what's wrong with the government and the legal system and loves to put the world to rights at every opportunity.

Cancer Ox

Oxen born under the sign of Cancer can go very far indeed, not through the application of brainpower although they are by no means unintelligent, but through the skills they have at their fingertips. These subjects are the craftsmen of the universe. Diligent, painstaking, and precise, they are incapable of bodging any practical task they undertake. They will spend hours and hours honing whatever craft has taken their fancy until they reach what looks to others like the peak of perfection. The Cancer Ox won't accept this of course. He can detect the minutest flaw in his own handiwork, but when he is finally forced to hand it over, everyone else is delighted with his efforts. Many artists, potters and sculptors are born under this sign.

Leo Ox

When the Lion of Leo meets the enormous strength of the Ox, the result is a formidable individual, indeed. Annoy or mock these powerful types at your peril. And anyone who dares to pick a fight with the Lion-Ox is likely to come out of it very badly. Most of the time, however, Leo is a friendly lion bringing confidence and a more relaxed attitude to the unbending Ox. These types are more broad-minded and open-hearted than the usual Oxen. They have been known to enjoy parties and once tempted into the limelight they may even find it's not as bad as they feared. In fact, secretly, they're having a ball.

Virgo Ox

Oxen born under the sign of Virgo tend to be very caring types. Though they show their feelings in practical ways and shun sloppy, emotional displays you can rely on an Ox born under Virgo to comfort the sick, help the old folk and notice if anyone in the neighborhood needs assistance. Florence Nightingale could have been a Virgo Ox. The unsentimental but immensely useful and humane work she did for her sick soldiers is typical of these types. They make excellent nurses and careworkers, forever plumping pillows, smoothing sheets and knowing just the right touches to bring comfort where it is needed. On a personal level, these subjects are inclined to be critical and easily irritated by the small failings of others, but their bark is worse than their bite. Their kindness shines through.

Libra Ox

Generally speaking the down to earth Ox has little time for putting on the charm. As far as Ox is concerned, people either like you or they don't, and it's not worth worrying about it either way. There's no point in wasting valuable time trying to bend your personality to accommodate the whims of others. Yet when the Ox is born under the sign of Libra, this trait is modified somewhat. Libra people just can't help having charm even if they are Oxen and therefore express that charm more brusquely than usual. The Libran Ox glides effortlessly through life, pleasing others without even realizing it. These types are sympathetic and like to help those in need wherever possible. Try to take advantage of their good nature or trick them with an untrue sob story, though, and they will never forgive you.

Scorpio Ox

The typical Ox is notoriously difficult to get to know, and when that Ox happens to be born under the secretive sign of Scorpio, you might as well give up and go home. You'll learn nothing from this creature unless he has some special reason for telling you. Stubborn and silent, these types are very deep indeed; they care nothing for the opinions of others and follow their own impenetrable hearts come what may. However, win the love of one of these unique subjects, and you have a very rare prize indeed. You will unlock a devotion and passion that you have probably never experienced before and will probably never experience again. This is a strangely compelling combination.

Sagittarius Ox

The Ox born under Sagittarius is a more carefree type than his brothers and sisters. Something of the free spirit of the horse touches these subjects, and while there is no chance of them kicking up their heels or doing anything remotely irresponsible, they at least understand these temptations in others and take a more relaxed view of life. The Ox born under Sagittarius is ambitious but independent. These types don't like to be told what to do and are probably more suited to being self-employed than working for others. They are more easy-going than a lot of Oxen and for this reason attract a wider range of friends. Like their Gemini cousins, they might even hazard a joke from time to time. All in all, the Ox born under Sagittarius gets more fun out of life.

Capricorn Ox

Unlike his Sagittarian brother, the Ox born under Capricorn takes himself and life very seriously indeed. These types usually do very well in material terms and often end up in positions of authority; yet if they're not careful, they can look burned out. With good reason. Capricorn Oxen have never learned how to relax, and they see life as a struggle; consequently, for them, it is. Yet they have much to be glad for. They are great savers for a rainy day, and so they never have to worry about unpaid bills, their capacity for hard work is so enormous they can hardly help but achieve a great deal, and before very long they find themselves well off and regarded with respect by everyone in the community. If these types could only manage to unwind, be gentle with themselves and enjoy their success, they could be very happy indeed.

Aquarius Ox

The Ox has never been a flashy sign. These types believe actions speak louder than words, and they like to beaver away without drawing attention to themselves. When this trait is coupled with the slightly introverted though idealistic nature of Aquarius, you get a quiet, complex character who prefers to work behind the scenes and turns modest when the limelight is switched on. Never known for his verbal dexterity, the Ox born under Aquarius can suddenly turn into a persuasive orator when a humanitarian cause sparks unexpected passion. These types make loyal, faithful companions to those who take the trouble to understand them and their intelligence and dogged persistence makes them invaluable as researchers, political assistants and private secretaries.

Pisces Ox

Few Oxen can be described as fey, changeable creatures but those that come the closest will be found under the sign of Pisces. Pisces brings an emotional, artistic quality to the steadfast Ox. These types are loving, faithful and true, yet it is often difficult to guess what they are thinking. Of all the Ox family, Pisces Oxen are likely to be the most moody and yet in many ways also the most creative. The Ox input lends strength and stamina to more delicate Pisces constitutions, enabling them to accomplish far more than other Pisces subjects. Just leave them alone until they're ready to face the world.

Tiger

Aries Tiger

Another combination which could be potentially explosive but in this case, energetic Aries adds force and power to the Tiger's humanitarian instincts while the Tiger's unworldly nature curbs Aries materialistic streak. These types really could change the world for the better if they put their minds to it. They are kind and thoughtful, and while they might be impatient at times, they quickly regret any harsh words spoken in the heat of the moment.

Taurus Tiger

Taurus Tigers are tremendous achievers. The strength of the zodiac bull added to the fire of the Tiger produces a truly formidable individual who can do almost anything to which he sets his mind. These types often end up making a great deal of money. They have to work hard for all their gains, but this doesn't worry them at all. They also take a great deal of pleasure in spending their hard-earned cash. They like to share what they've got, and this gives them such childish joy that no-one begrudges them their good fortune.

Gemini Tiger

The quicksilver mind of Gemini adds zing and extra flexibility to the Tiger's powerful individualism. These Tigers are blessed with minds which overflow with brilliant ideas. They are creative and often artistic too, so they're capable of wonderful achievements. Their only drawback is that they possess almost too much of a good thing. They have so many ideas that they tend to zoom off at a tangent onto a new task before they have completed the one on which they were working.

Cancer Tiger

These Tigers are immensely clever but a little more retiring than the usual bold, brave terror of the jungle. No Tiger is timid, but Cancer has the effect of quietening the more reckless excesses of the Tiger and allowing a little caution to creep into the blend. They still like a challenge but will opt for something a little less physically demanding than other Tigers. These types are more able to fit into society and tolerate authority better than other Tigers, and for this reason they often do well in their careers.

Leo Tiger

What would you get if you crossed a lion with a tiger? A very wild beast indeed. Some sort of striped wonder of the world no doubt! Leo Tigers certainly make their mark. Tigers are big, beautiful, fearless personalities who crave the limelight and love to be noticed. They believe in doing good deeds, but they like to be noticed doing them. These are not the types of which anonymous benefactors are made. When the Leo Tiger raises money for charity, he likes to make sure the world's press are gathered to record the occasion if at all possible. Yet his heart's in the right place. Let these Tigers have their share of praise, and they will work wonders for others.

Virgo Tiger

The Virgo Tiger is quite a different beast. Virgo accentuates the Tiger's already well-developed sense of justice. These types cannot rest until wrongdoers have got their just deserts. They often go into professions involving the law and the police force. They are immensely self-disciplined and have very high standards. Totally trustworthy and effective, they can sometimes be a little difficult to live with. They are not unkind; it's just that they expect everyone else to be as perfect as they are themselves. Yet Virgo adds attention-to-detail to Tiger's passion to change the world, and the combination creates a character who really could make a lasting difference.

Libra Tiger

Laidback Libra brings quite a different quality to the Tiger. Tiger's intensity is softened by pure Libra charm, and the result is a Tiger of unrivalled compassion and magnetism. Libra Tigers often end up in the caring professions where people flock to them with relief. These Tigers want to help, and Libra gives them the ability to understand just what people need and when. You'd never catch a Libra Tiger helping an old lady across the road who didn't wish to go. Libra Tiger would realize at once that the woman was waiting for a bus, would stand with her to keep her company, help her on when the vehicle arrived and make sure the driver put her off at the right stop. No wonder these Tigers are so well-loved wherever they go.

Scorpio Tiger

Crossing a Scorpion with a Tiger is a very tricky proposition. These types mean well, but they are often misunderstood. Scorpio brings a tremendous depth of feeling to the Tiger's reforming instincts, but this sometimes causes them to put tremendous effort into the wrong causes with alarming results. These types can be very quick-tempered, and they may nurse a grudge for a long time. They never forgive disloyalty, and they never forget. It would be a serious mistake to make an enemy of a Scorpio Tiger – but once this individual becomes a friend, they'll be loyal for life.

Sagittarius Tiger

Another charmer, the Sagittarius Tiger is nevertheless likely to hit the road at the slightest opportunity. These types are wanderers, and no matter how much they seem to enjoy company, they enjoy moving on even more. They can't bear working for other people and do far better being self-employed. The travel industry would suit them perfectly. Impossible to cage in or pin down – don't even try – the only way to have a happy relationship with a Sagittarius Tiger is to make them feel free at all times.

Capricorn Tiger

Steady Capricorn lends a prudent touch to the impulsive Tiger, and these types are the Tigers most likely to stop and think before rushing off to save the rain forest. They still enjoy improving the world, but they check travel arrangements, make sure they have got sufficient funds and do a bit of research online first. These are not party animals. While they enjoy company, they prefer serious discussion to frivolous small talk and much as they enjoy travel they appreciate the comfort of home. These Tigers like to develop their theories from the depths of their favorite armchair beside their own cozy hearth.

Aquarius Tiger

When idealistic Aquarius meets idealistic Tiger, you have to hang onto that long tiger tail to keep these subjects, feet on the ground. These types really do have their heads in the clouds and are totally unpredictable. Once a worthwhile cause presents itself, they will rush off immediately without a thought to the consequences. Convention is of no interest to them. They couldn't care less what other people think. They go through life guided entirely by a strong inner sense of right and wrong. If it's right, they know it without a shadow of a doubt; if it's wrong, they will not do it no matter what anyone says. This attitude can get them into a lot of trouble, but other signs sneakily admire their courage. People may not agree with Aquarius Tiger, but no one can doubt his integrity.

Pisces Tiger

One of Tiger's failings is a tendency to be indecisive without warning, and this trait is heightened in Pisces Tigers. These types are anxious to do the right thing; it's just that sometimes it's very difficult to know what that right thing is. There are so many alternatives. Pisces Tiger is kind and gentle and apt to get sentimental at times. They want to save the world, but they'd like someone alongside to help them – though not too many. Despite their indecision, they usually end up heading in the right direction in the end. Yet, even when they've achieved a great deal, they still agonize over whether they could have done even more.

Rabbit

Aries Rabbit

This is a very dynamic Rabbit. When powerful Aries injects a streak of energy into that cultured Rabbit personality, the result is a wonderfully clever individual who glides effortlessly to success. Although at times Aries Rabbit has an attack of over-cautiousness, these types are usually bolder than the average bunny and achieve much where other Rabbits might run away. Occasionally, these Rabbits will even take a gamble, and this is worthwhile as it usually pays off for them.

Taurus Rabbit

The Taurus Rabbit really does feel his home is his castle. He is not unduly interested in his career, but he is likely to turn his home into an art form. Brilliant entertainers, these types guarantee their lucky guests will enjoy all the creature comforts possible. They often marry later in life than average, but when they do, they work at the relationship. Providing they choose another home bird, they are likely to be very happy.

Gemini Rabbit

All Rabbits are natural diplomats, but the Gemini Rabbit really is the star of them all. So skilled a communicator is this creature, so expert at people management that a career in the diplomatic service, politics, psychology or even advertising is an option. Never lost for words, these types can persuade anyone to do almost anything. As a result, they are usually very successful. Once they harness their enviable skills to a worthwhile career, they can go far.

Cancer Rabbit

Cancer Rabbits are gentle, kindly souls. They like to be surrounded by pleasant company and prefer to have few demands put upon them. They don't really take to business life and find many professions too abrasive. On the other hand, they find working for themselves too stressful a venture to be considered seriously. They are happiest in a peaceful, routine environment where they can make steady progress, but really their hearts are at home. Home is where they express themselves.

Leo Rabbit

Leo Rabbits, on the other hand, are usually very popular with a wide circle of friends. Extrovert Leo gives Rabbit a strong dose of confidence and flair, and when these qualities are added to Rabbit's people skills, a radiant, magnetic individual is born. Leo Rabbits adore parties where they shine. They are always elegant and beautifully turned out and have a knack of putting others at their ease. These Rabbits climb the ladder of success very quickly.

Virgo Rabbit

Virgo Rabbits have a lot on their minds. The natural cautiousness of the Rabbit is heightened by the same quality in Virgo, and these Rabbits tend to be born worriers. They are masters of detail but, unfortunately, this often leads them to make mountains out of molehills. They are very talented creatures but too often fail to make the best use of their gifts because they spend so much time worrying about all the things that could go wrong. If they can learn to relax and take the odd risk now and then, they will go far.

Libra Rabbit

Art-loving Libra blends easily into the cultured sign of the Rabbit. These types love to learn more about beautiful things, and they like to share their knowledge with others. They are so good with people that they can convey information effortlessly and make the dullest subject sound interesting. These types are often gifted teachers and lecturers though they would find difficult inner-city schools too traumatic. Give these types willing and interested pupils, and they blossom.

Scorpio Rabbit

Rabbits tend to be discreet people, and Scorpio Rabbits are the most tight-lipped of the lot. Scorpio Rabbits have a lot of secrets, and they enjoy keeping them. It gives them a wonderful feeling of superiority to think that they know things others don't. They have many secret ambitions too, and they don't like to speak of them in case others are pessimistic and pour scorn on their plans. So it is the Scorpio Rabbit who is most likely to surprise everyone by suddenly reaching an amazing goal that no-one even knew he was aiming for.

Sagittarius Rabbit

Sporty Sagittarius brings a whole new dimension to the art-loving Rabbit. Rabbits are often indoor creatures, but Sagittarian Rabbits are much more adventurous in the open air than the usual bunny. They are sensuous and fun and attract many friends. They are also versatile and can turn their hands to several different careers if necessary. They like to get out and about more than most Rabbits and they are usually very successful.

Capricorn Rabbit

Capricorn Rabbits are great family folk. They firmly believe the family is the bedrock of life, and they work hard to keep their relations happy and together. The Capricorn Rabbit home is the center of numerous clan gatherings throughout the year and weddings, birthdays, anniversaries and christenings are very important to them. Capricorn Rabbit will never forget the dates. These types are particularly interested in the past and will enjoy researching a family tree going back generations. If it ever crosses their minds that the rest of the tribe seems to leave all the donkey work to Capricorn Rabbit, he'd never say so. And, in truth, he doesn't really mind. There's nothing he loves more than having his family around him.

Aquarius Rabbit

The Aquarius Rabbit is a contradictory creature being both cautious and curious at the same time. These types crave security and love, and yet they have a great longing to find out more about everything around them. Fascinated by art, science and new inventions they love to potter about in book shops and tinker in the shed at home. Once they get an idea in their head, they can't rest until they have experimented with it, frequently forgetting to eat while they work. They need love and understanding.

Pisces Rabbit

The Pisces Rabbit is another bunny who needs a lot of understanding. Often gifted artistically they can sometimes be stubborn and awkward for no apparent reason. Yet when they are in the right frame of mind, they can charm the birds off the trees. It takes them a long time to make a friend, but when they do, it is a friend for life. The Pisces Rabbit home is full of beautiful things, and these subjects love to invite their most trusted friends to come and enjoy the magic.

Dragon

Aries Dragon

The Dragon is already a powerful sign, but when the lively influence of Aries is added, you have a positively devastating individual. These are the types that others either love or loathe. Strong, confident people can cope happily with the Aries Dragon, but more timid souls are terrified. The Aries Dragon himself is quite unaware of the reaction he causes. He goes busily on his way oblivious of the earthquakes all around him. These types have to guard against arrogance, particularly since they have quite a lot to be arrogant about. They also have a tendency to get bored easily and move on to new projects without completing the old, which is a pity since they can accomplish much if they persevere.

Taurus Dragon

There is something magnificent about the Taurus Dragon. Large, expansive types, they move easily around the social scene spreading bonhomie wherever they go. Not the most sensitive of individuals, they find it difficult to assess the moods of others and assume everyone else feels the same way they do. Should it be brought to their attention that someone is unhappy, however, they will move heaven and earth to cheer them up. These types are reliable and conscientious and always keep their promises.

Gemini Dragon

Dragons may not have the quickest minds in the Chinese zodiac, but Gemini Dragons are speedier than most. They are jovial types with a brilliant sense of humor. In fact, they can cleverly joke others into doing what they want. These types have no need for physical force to get their own way; they use laughter instead. At times, Gemini Dragons can be almost devious, which is unusual for a Dragon but nobody really minds their schemes. They give everyone such a good time on the way it's worth doing what they want for the sheer entertainment.

Cancer Dragon

Cautious Cancer and flamboyant Dragon make a surprisingly good combination. Cancer holds Dragon back where he might go too far, while Dragon endows the Crab with exuberance and style. These types like to help others make the most of themselves, but they are also high achievers in their own right. Without upsetting anyone, Cancer Dragons tend to zoom to the top faster than most.

Leo Dragon

This Dragon is so dazzling you need sunglasses to look at him. The proud, glorious Lion combined with the magnificent Dragon is an extraordinary combination, and it's fortunate it only comes around once every twelve years. Too many of such splendid creatures would be hard to take. Leo Dragons really do have star quality, and they know it. They demand to be the center of attention and praise is like oxygen to them – they can't live without it. Yet they have generous hearts, and if anyone is in trouble, Leo Dragon will be the first to rush to their assistance.

Virgo Dragon

Unusually for a Dragon, the Virgo variety can get quite aggressive if crossed, but this doesn't often happen as very few people would dare take on such a daunting beast. These types are immensely clever in business. They steadily add acquisition to shrewd acquisition until they end up seriously rich. They are wilier than most Dragons who have a surprisingly naive streak, and they make the most of it. These types just can't help becoming successful in whatever they undertake.

Libra Dragon

Dragons are not usually too bothered about trifles such as fine clothes and wallpaper. In fact, some older, more absent-minded Dragons have been known to go shopping in their slippers having forgotten to take them off. The exception is the Dragon born under the sign of Libra. These types are more down to earth and see the sense in putting on a good show for others. They take the trouble to choose smart clothes and keep them looking that way at all times. They are also more intuitive and are not easily fooled by others.

Scorpio Dragon

Handling money is not a Dragon strong point, but the Scorpio variety has more ability in this direction than most. Scorpio Dragons enjoy amassing cash. Rather like their legendary namesakes who hoard treasure in their lairs, Scorpio Dragons like to build substantial nest-eggs and keep them close at hand where they can admire them regularly. These types can also be a little stingy financially, not out of true meanness but simply because they don't like to see their carefully guarded heap diminish in size. Once they understand the importance of a purchase, however, they can be just as generous as their brothers and sisters.

Sagittarius Dragon

When Sagittarius joins the Dragon, the combination produces a real livewire, a true daredevil. The antics of the Sagittarius Dragon, when young, will give their mothers nightmares and later drive their partners to drink. These types can't resist a challenge, particularly a dangerous one. They will climb mountain peaks, leap off diffs on a hang-glider and try a spot of bungee-jumping to enliven a dull moment. It's no good expecting these types to sit down with a good book; they just can't keep still. However, surrounded by friends, dashing from one perilous venture to the next, the Sagittarius Dragon is one of the happiest people around.

Capricorn Dragon

The Capricorn Dragon looks back at his Sagittarian brother in horror. He simply can't understand the need for such pranks. Being Dragons, these types are bold, but the influence of Capricorn ensures that they are never foolhardy. They look before they leap and occasionally miss a good deal because they stop to check the fine print. They are not the most intuitive of creatures, but show them a needy soul and they will efficiently do whatever's necessary to help. The Capricorn Dragon is a highly effective creature.

Aquarius Dragon

Happy go lucky types, the Aquarius Dragons are usually surrounded by people. Honest and hardworking, they will put in just as much effort for very little cash as they will for a great deal. If someone asks them to do a job and they agree to do it, they will move heaven and earth to fulfil their obligations even if it is not in their best interests to do so. However, they're not suited to routine, and if a task doesn't interest them, they will avoid it at all costs no matter how well paid it might be. Not particularly interested in money for its own sake, these types are sociable and easy to get along with. They are often highly talented in some way.

Pisces Dragon

Pisces Dragons, on the other hand, are surprisingly good with cash. Despite their often vague, good-humored exteriors these types have excellent financial brains and seem to know just what to do to increase their savings. They are first in the queue when bargains are to be found, and they seem to sense what the next money-making trend is going to be before anyone else has thought of it. These types often end up quite wealthy and excel, particularly, in artistic fields.

Snake

Aries Snake

Generally speaking, Snakes tend to lack energy, so the influence of dynamic Aries is very welcome indeed. These subjects are highly intelligent, well-motivated and never leave anything unfinished. They are achievers and will not give up until they reach their goal – which they invariably do. Nothing can stand in the way of Aries Snakes, and they reach the top of whatever tree they climb.

Taurus Snake

In contrast, the sensuous Taurus Snake really can't be bothered with all that hard work. Taurus Snakes have great ability, but they will only do as much as is necessary to acquire the lifestyle they desire, and then they like to sit back and enjoy it. Tremendous sun worshippers, the Taurus Snakes would be quite happy to be on a permanent holiday, providing the accommodation was a five-star hotel with a fabulous restaurant.

Gemini Snake

The Gemini Snake can be a slippery customer. A brilliant brain, linked to a shrewd but amusing tongue, these types can run rings around almost everybody. They can scheme and manipulate if it suits them and pull off all sorts of audacious tricks but having achieved much, they tend to get bored and lose interest, giving up on the brink of great things. This often leads to conflict with business associates who cannot understand such contradictory behavior. Insane they call it. Suicidal. The Gemini Snake just shrugs and moves on.

Cancer Snake

The Snake born under the sign of Cancer is a more conventional creature. These types will at least do all that is required of them and bring their formidable Snake brains to bear on the task in hand. They are gifted researchers, historians and archaeologists – any career which involves deep concentration and patient study. But the Cancer Snake must take care to mix with cheerful people since left to himself he has a tendency for melancholy. Warmth, laughter, and plenty of rest transforms the Cancer Snake and allows those unique talents to blossom.

Leo Snake

The Leo Snake is a very seductive creature. Beautifully dressed, sparklingly magnetic, few people can take their eyes off these types, and they know it. All Snakes are sensuous, but the Snake born under the sign of Leo is probably the most sensuous of the lot. Never short of admirers, these types are not eager to settle down. Why should they when they're having such a good time? Late in life, the Leo Snake may consent to get married if their partner can offer them a good enough life. If not, these types are quite content to go it alone – probably because they are never truly on their own. They collect willing followers right into old age.

Virgo Snake

The Virgo Snake is another fascinating combination. Highly intuitive and wildly passionate, the Virgo Snake is all elegant understatement on the outside and erotic abandon on the inside. The opposite sex is mesmerized by this intriguing contradiction and just can't stay away. Virgo Snakes can achieve success in their careers if they put their minds to it, but often they are having too much fun flirting and flitting from one lover to the next. Faithfulness is not their strong point, but they are so sexy they get away with murder.

Libra Snake

When you see a top model slinking sinuously down the catwalk, she could very well be a Libra Snake. Snakes born under this sign are the most elegant and stylish of the lot. They may not be conventionally good looking, but they will turn heads wherever they go. These types really understand clothes and could make a plastic bin-liner look glamorous just by putting it on. Somehow they have the knack of stepping off a transatlantic flight without a crease and driving an open-topped sports car without ruffling their hair. No-one knows quite how they achieve these feats, and Libra Snake isn't telling.

Scorpio Snake

The Snake born under Scorpio is destined to have a complicated life. These types enjoy plots and intrigues, particularly of a romantic nature and spend endless hours devising schemes and planning subterfuge. That ingenious Snake brain is capable of brewing up the most elaborate scams, and there's nothing Scorpio Snake loves more than watching all the parts fall into place. But schemes have a knack of going wrong, and schemers have to change their plans and change them again to cope with each new contingency as it arises. If he's not careful, the Scorpio Snake can become hopelessly embroiled in his own plot.

Sagittarius Snake

Traditionally other signs are wary of the Snake and tend to hold back a little from them without knowing why. When the Snake is born under Sagittarius, however, the subject seems more approachable than most. Sagittarian Snakes sooner or later become recognized for their wisdom and down to earth good sense and people flock to them for advice. Without ever intending to, the Sagittarius Snake could end up as something of a guru attracting eager acolytes desperate to learn more.

Capricorn Snake

The Snake born under Capricorn is more ambitious than the average serpent. These types will reach for the stars and grasp them. Obstacles just melt away when faced with the dual-beam of Capricorn Snake intelligence and quiet persistence. These Snakes are good providers and more dependable than most Snakes. They often end up surrounded by all the trappings of success, but they accomplish this so quietly, no one can quite work out how they managed it.

Aquarius Snake

Another highly intuitive Snake. Independent but people-loving Aquarius endows the serpent with greater social skills than usual. These types attract many friends, and they have the ability to understand just how others are feeling without them having to say a word. These Snakes have particularly enquiring minds, and they can't pass a museum or book shop without going in to browse. Born researchers, they love to dig and delve into whatever subject has taken their fancy, no matter how obscure. Quite often, they discover something valuable by accident.

Pisces Snake

Pisces Snakes tend to live on their nerves even more than most. These types are friendly up to a point, but they hate disagreements and problems and withdraw when things look unpleasant. They are sexy and sensuous and would much prefer a quiet evening with just one special person than a wild party. In the privacy of their bedroom, anything goes, and Pisces Snakes reveal the naughty side of their characters. No one would guess from the understated elegance of their exteriors what an erotic creature the Pisces Snake really is.

Horse

Aries Horse

Overflowing with energy the Aries Horse just can't sit still for long. These types just have to find an outlet for their phenomenal vitality. They are hardworking, hard-playing, and usually highly popular. Less fun-loving signs might be accused of being workaholics but not the Aries Horse. People born under this sign devote enormous amounts of time to their careers but still have so much spare capacity there is plenty left over for their friends. They always do well in their chosen profession.

Taurus Horse

The Taurus Horse can be a trickier creature. Charming yet logical, he has a very good brain and is not afraid to use it. The only problem is that without warning the Taurus Horse can turn from flighty and fun to immensely stubborn and even an earthquake wouldn't shift him from an entrenched position. Yet treated with understanding and patience, the Taurus Horse can be coaxed to produce wonderful achievements.

Gemini Horse

Gemini types are easily bored, and when they are born in the freedom-loving year of the Horse, this trait tends to be accentuated. Unless their attention is caught and held almost instantly, Gemini Horse subjects kick up their heels and gallop off to find more fun elsewhere. For this reason, they often find it difficult to hold on to a job, and they change careers frequently. Yet once they discover a subject about which they can feel passionate, they employ the whole of their considerable talent and will zoom to the top in record time.

Cancer Horse

The Cancer Horse is a lovable creature with a great many friends. These types tend to lack confidence and need a lot of praise and nurturing, but with the right leadership, they will move mountains. Some signs find them difficult to understand because the Cancer Horse loves to be surrounded by a crowd yet needs a lot of alone time too. Misjudge the mood, and the Cancer Horse can seem bafflingly unfriendly. Yet, stay the course, and these subjects become wonderfully loyal friends.

Leo Horse

People born under the star sign of Leo will be the first to admit they like to show off and when they are also born in the year of the Horse, they enjoy showing off all the more. These types love nothing better than strutting around rocking designer outfits while others look on in admiration. They are not so interested in home decor; it's their own personal appearance which counts most. The Leo Horse would much rather invest time and money boosting their image than shoving their earnings into a bank account to gather dust.

Virgo Horse

Virgo types can be a little solemn and over-devoted to duty, but when they are born in the year of the Horse, they are endowed with a welcome streak of equine frivolity. The Virgo Horse loves to party. He will make sure his work is completed first of course, but once the office door clicks shut behind him, the Virgo Horse really knows how to let his hair down.

Libra Horse

The Libra Horse is another true charmer. Friends and acquaintances by the score fill the address books of these types, and their diaries are crammed with appointments. Honest, trustworthy and helpful, other people can't help gravitating to them. Oddly enough, despite their gregarious nature, these types are also very independent. Sometimes too independent for their own good. They are excellent at giving advice to others but find it almost impossible to take advice themselves.

Scorpio Horse

The Scorpio Horse is a real thrill seeker. These types enjoy life's pleasures, particularly passionate pleasures and go all out to attain them. There is no middle road with the Scorpio Horse. These are all or nothing types. They fling themselves into the project of the moment wholeheartedly or not at all. They tend to see things in black and white and believe others are either for them or against them. In serious moments, the Scorpio Horse subscribes to some surprising conspiracy theories, but mostly they keep these ideas to themselves.

Sagittarius Horse

The star sign of Sagittarius is the sign of the Centaur – half-man half-horse – and when these types are born in the year of the Horse, the equine tendencies are so strong they practically have four hooves. Carefree country-lovers these subjects can't bear to be penned in and never feel totally happy until they are out of doors in some wide-open space. They crave fresh air and regular exercise and do best in joint activities. As long as they can spend enough time out of doors, Sagittarius Horses are blessed with glowing good health.

Capricorn Horse

The Capricorn Horse is a canny beast. These types are great savers. They manage to have fun on a shoestring and stash away every spare penny at the same time. They are prepared to work immensely hard provided the pay is good, and they have a remarkable knack of finding just the right job to make the most of their earning power. The Capricorn Horse likes a good time, and he will never be poor.

Aquarius Horse

When Aquarius meets the Horse, it results in a very curious creature. These types admit to enquiring minds; other less charitable signs might call them nosey parkers. Call them what you may, subjects born under this sign need to know and discover. They often become inventors, and they have a weakness for new gadgets and the latest technology. The Aquarius Horse can be wildly impractical and annoy partners by frittering cash away on their latest obsession. They also tend to fill their living space with peculiar objects from junk shops and car boot sales, which they intend to upcycle into useful treasures. Somehow, they seldom get round to finishing the project.

Pisces Horse

Artistic Pisces adds an unusual dimension to the physical Horse, who normally has little time for cultural frills and foibles. These types are great home entertainers and often gifted cooks as well. They invite a group of friends around at the slightest excuse and can conjure delicious snacks and drinks from the most unpromising larders. They adore company and get melancholy if left alone too long.

Goat

Aries Goat

Normally mild and unassuming, the Goat can become almost argumentative when born under the star sign of Aries. Though friendly and very seldom cross, the Aries Goat will suddenly adopt an unexpectedly stubborn position and stick to it unreasonably even when it's obvious he is wrong. Despite this, these types are blessed with sunny natures and are quickly forgiven. They don't bear a grudge and have no idea – after the awkwardness – that anything unpleasant occurred.

Taurus Goat

Like his Aries cousin, the Taurus Goat can turn stubborn too. These types have a very long fuse. Most people would assume they did not have a temper because it is so rarely displayed. But make them truly angry, and they will explode. Small they may be, but a raging Goat can be a fearful sight. On the other hand, these Goats are more likely to have a sweet tooth than their cousins, so if you do upset them, a choccy treat could work wonders in making amends.

Gemini Goat

The Goat born under Gemini is a terrible worrier. These types seem to use their active minds to dream up all the troubles and problems that could result from every single action. Naturally, this renders decision-making almost impossible. They dither and rethink and ponder until finally someone else makes up their mind for them, at which point they are quite happy. In fact, if the Gemini Goat never had to make another decision, she would be a blissfully content creature.

Cancer Goat

Gentle, soft-hearted and kind, the Cancer Goat is a friend to all in need. These types would give their last penny to a homeless beggar in the street, and they always have a shoulder ready should anyone need to cry on it. Yet they can also be surprisingly moody for what appears to be no reason at all, and this characteristic can be baffling to their friends. No point in wasting time asking what's wrong, they find it difficult to explain. Just wait for the clouds to pass.

Leo Goat

The Leo Goat is a very fine specimen. Warm, friendly and more extrovert than her quieter Goat cousins, she seems to have the confidence other Goats often lack. Look more closely though, and you can find all is not quite as it seems. Frequently, that self-assured appearance is merely a well-presented 'front'. Back in the privacy of their own home, the bold Leo Goat can crumble. In truth, these types are easily hurt.

Virgo Goat

Outwardly vague and preoccupied, the Virgo Goat can turn unexpectedly fussy. These types are easy-going, but they can't stand messy homes, mud in their car or sweet wrappers lying around. Yet they would be genuinely surprised if anyone accused them of being pernickety. They believe they are laid back and good-humored, which they are. Just don't drop chewing gum on their front path, that's all, and take your shoes off at the door.

Libra Goat

The Libra Goat is obliging to the point of self-sacrifice. These types are truly nice people. Generous with their time as well as their possessions. Unfortunately, their good nature is sometimes exploited by the unscrupulous. The Libra Goat will wear itself out in the service of those in distress, will refuse to hear a bad word about anyone and will remain loyal to friends despite the most intense provocation. The Libra Goat lives to please.

Scorpio Goat

Scorpio Goats are among the most strong-willed of all the Goats. They like to go their own way and hate to have others tell them what to do. They don't mind leaving irksome chores and duties to others, but woe betides anyone who tries to interfere with the Scorpio Goat's pet project.

At first sight, they may appear preoccupied and have their heads in the clouds, but beneath that vague exterior, their sharp eyes miss very little. Don't underestimate the Scorpio Goat.

Sagittarius Goat

Sagittarius lends an adventurous streak to the normally cautious Goat make-up, and these types tend to take far more risks than their cousins born at other times of the year. While they still enjoy being taken care of, the Sagittarius Goat prefers cosseting on his return from adventures, not instead of them. These types are often good in business and amaze everyone by doing 'extremely well' apparently by accident.

Capricorn Goat

The Capricorn Goat, in contrast, is a very cautious creature. Danger beckons at every turn and security is top of their list of priorities. This Goat can never get to sleep until every door and window has been locked and secured. Should they find themselves staying in a hotel, Capricorn Goats will often drag a chair in front of the bedroom door, just in case. These types are difficult to get to know because it takes a while to win their trust, but once they become friends they will be loyal forever and despite their caution – or sensible outlook as they'd call it – they can be very successful.

Aquarius Goat

The Aquarius Goat tends to leap about from one high-minded project to the next. These well-meaning types might be manning a soup kitchen one day and devising a scheme to combat climate change the next. Their grand plans seldom come to fruition because they find the practical details so difficult to put into operation but should they link up with an organizational genius they could achieve great things.

Pisces Goat

The Pisces Goat is a very sensitive soul. These types are often highly gifted, and their best course of action is to find someone to take care of them as soon as possible so that they can get on with cultivating their talents. Left to themselves Pisces Goats will neglect their physical needs, failing to cook proper meals or dress warmly in cold weather. With the right guidance, however, they can work wonders.

Monkey

Aries Monkey

These cheeky types have a charm that is quite irresistible. Energetic and mischievous they adore parties and social gatherings of any kind. They crop up on every guest list because they are so entertaining. The Aries Monkey is a font of funny stories and silly jokes but seldom stands still for long. Friends of the Aries Monkey are often frustrated as their popular companion is so in demand it's difficult to pin her down for a catch-up.

Taurus Monkey

The Monkey born under the star sign of Taurus has a little more weight in his character. These types take life a shade more seriously than their delightfully frivolous cousins. Not that the Taurus Monkey is ever a stick-in-the-mud. It's just that business comes before pleasure with these types, although only just, and the business that catches their eye is not necessarily what others would call business. Taurus Monkey is as captivated by creating a useful container out of an old coffee jar as checking out a balance sheet.

Gemini Monkey

The Gemini Monkey Is a true comedian. Incredibly quick-witted, these types only have to open their mouths, and everyone around them is in stitches. If Oscar Wilde was not a Gemini Monkey, he should have been. People born under this sign could easily make a career in the comedy field if they can be bothered to make enough attempts. Truth is they're just as happy entertaining their friends as a theatre full of people.

Cancer Monkey

These types have a gentler side to their characters. Cancer Monkey's love to tinker with machinery and see how things work. They tend to take things to pieces and then forget to put them together again. They are easily hurt, however, if someone complains about this trait. They genuinely intend to put things right. It is just that somehow they never manage to get round to it, and they never realize that this is a trait they repeat over and over again.

Leo Monkey

The Leo Monkey is a highly adaptable creature. He can be all things to all men while still retaining his own unique personality. Popular, amusing and fond of practical jokes these types are welcome wherever they go. They can sometimes get rather carried away with the sound of their own voices and end up being rather tactless, but such is their charm that everyone forgives them. Occasionally, a practical joke can go too far, but kind-hearted Leo Monkey is horrified if anyone feels hurt, and instantly apologizes.

Virgo Monkey

The Virgo Monkey could be a great inventor. The Monkey's natural ingenuity blends with Virgo's patience and fussiness over detail to create a character with the ideas to discover something new and the tenacity to carry on until it is perfected. If they could curb their impulse to rush on to the next brilliant idea when the last is complete, and turned their intention instead to marketing, they could make a fortune.

Libra Monkey

The Monkey born under the sign of Libra is actually a force to be reckoned with though no-one would ever guess it. These types are lovable and fun and have a knack of getting other people to do what they want without even realizing they've been talked into it. In fact, Libran Monkeys are first-class manipulators but so skilled at their craft that nobody minds. These types could get away with murder.

Scorpio Monkey

Normally, the Monkey is a real chatterbox, but when Scorpio is added to the mix, you have a primate with the unusual gift of discretion right alongside his natural loquaciousness. These types will happily gossip all day long, but if they need to keep a secret, they are able to do so, to the grave if necessary. Scorpio Monkey could be an actor or a spy – and play each role to perfection. 007 could well have been a Scorpio Monkey.

Sagittarius Monkey

These flexible, amorous, adventure-loving Monkeys add zing to any gathering. These are the guests with the mad-cap ideas who want to jump fully clothed into the swimming pool at midnight and think it terrific fun to see in the New Year on top of Ben Nevis. It's difficult to keep up with the Sagittarius Monkey, but it's certainly fun to try.

Capricorn Monkey

Capricorn Monkeys have their serious side, but they are also flirty types. These are the subjects who charm with ease and tease and joke their conquests into bed. The trouble is Capricorn Monkey often promises more than is deliverable. These types tire more easily than they realize, and can't always put their exciting schemes into action. This rarely stops them trying, of course.

Aquarius Monkey

The Aquarius Monkey is a particularly inventive creature and employs his considerable intellect in trying to discover new ways to save the world. These types often have a hard time in their early years as it takes them decades to realize that not everyone sees the importance of their passions as they do. But, once they understand a different approach is needed, they go on to accomplish much in later life.

Pisces Monkey

The Pisces Monkey can be a puzzling creature. These types are dreamy and amusing one minute and irritable and quick-tempered the next. They can go with the flow so far and then suddenly wonder why no-one can keep up with them when they decide to get a move on. They tend to lack quite so much humor when the joke is on themselves, but most of the time they are agreeable companions.

Rooster

Aries Rooster

Stand well back when confronted with an Aries Rooster. These types are one hundred percent go-getter, and nothing will stand in their way. Aries Rooster can excel at anything to which he puts his mind, and as he frequently puts his mind to business matters, he's likely to end up a billionaire. Think scarlet sports cars, ostentatious homes, and a personal helicopter or two – the owner is bound to be an Aries Rooster.

Taurus Rooster

The Taurus Rooster has a heart of gold but can come over as a bit of a bossy boots, particularly in financial matters. These types believe they have a unique understanding of money and accounts and are forever trying to get more sloppy signs to sharpen up in this department. Even if their manner rankles, it's worth listening to their advice. Annoyingly, they are often right.

Gemini Rooster

The Rooster born under the sign of Gemini would make a terrific private detective were it not for the fact that Roosters find it almost impossible to blend into the background. Gemini Roosters love to find out what's going on and have an uncanny ability to stumble on the one thing you don't wish them to know. They mean no harm, however, and once they find a suitable outlet for their talents, they will go far.

Cancer Rooster

The Rooster born under the sign of Cancer is often a fine-looking creature and knows it. These types are secretly rather vain and behind the scenes take great pains with their appearance. They would die rather than admit it, however, and like to give the impression that their wonderful style is no more than a happy accident. Though they cultivate a relaxed, easy-going manner, a bad hair day or a splash of mud on their new suede boots is enough to send them into a major sulk for hours.

Leo Rooster

Not everyone takes to the Leo Rooster. The Lion is a naturally proud, extrovert sign and when allied to the strutting Rooster, there is a danger of these types ending up as bossy exhibitionists. Yet they really have the kindest of hearts and will leap from their pedestals in an instant to comfort someone who seems upset. A word of warning – they should avoid excessive alcohol as these types can get merry on a sniff of a cider apple.

Virgo Rooster

The Virgo Rooster is a hardworking, dedicated creature, devoted to family, but in an undemonstrative way. Wind this bird up at your peril, however. These types have little sense of humor when it comes to taking a joke, and they will hold a grudge for months if they feel someone has made them look foolish. They hate to be laughed at.

Libra Rooster

The Libra Rooster likes to look good, have a fine home and share his considerable assets with his closest friends. These types enjoy admiration, but they are more subtle than Leo Roosters and don't demand it quite so openly. Libra Rooster is quite happy to give but does expect gratitude in return.

Scorpio Rooster

The Scorpio Rooster is a heroic creature. These types will defend a position to the death. In days of old, many a Scorpio Rooster will have got involved in a duel because these types cannot endure insults, will fight aggression with aggression and will not back down under any circumstances. Foolhardy they may appear, but there is something admirable about them nevertheless.

Sagittarius Rooster

The Sagittarius Rooster tends to be a little excitable and rash. These types are bold and brash and ready for anything. They love to travel and are desperate to see what's over the next hill and around the next bend. Born explorers' they never want to tread the conventional travel path. Let others holiday in Marbella if they wish. Sagittarius Rooster prefers a walking tour of Tibet.

Capricorn Rooster

Capricorn brings a steadying quality to the impulsive Rooster. These types like to achieve, consolidate, and then build again. They believe they are amassing a fortune for their family and they usually do. However, sometimes, their families would prefer a little less security and more attention. Best not to mention it to Capricorn Rooster though – this Rooster is likely to feel hurt and offended.

Aquarius Rooster

The Aquarius Rooster is frequently misunderstood. These types mean well but they tend to be impulsive and speak before they think, accidentally offending others when they do so. In fact, the Aquarius Rooster is a sensitive creature beneath that brash exterior and is easily hurt. If they can learn to count to ten before saying anything controversial, and maybe rephrase, they'd be amazed at how successful they'd become.

Pisces Rooster

The Pisces Rooster has a secret fear. He is terrified that one day he will be terribly poor. These types save hard to stave off that dreadful fate and will only feel totally relaxed when they have a huge nest egg behind them. Despite this, they manage to fall in and out of love regularly and often end up delighting their partners with the wonderful lifestyle they can create.

Dog

Aries Dog

The Aries Dog is a friendly type. Extrovert and sociable these subjects like a lively career and cheerful home life. They are not excessively materialistic, but they tend to make headway in the world without trying too hard. Aries Dog likes to get things done and will bound from one task to the next with energy and enthusiasm.

Taurus Dog

The Dog born under the star sign of Taurus is the most dependable creature in the world. Their word really is their bond, and they will never break a promise while there is breath in their body. They tend to be ultra-conservative with a small 'c'. The men are inclined to be chauvinists, and the women usually hold traditional views. They really do prefer to make their home and family their priority. They are loyal and kind, and people instinctively trust them.

Gemini Dog

The Gemini Dog, in contrast, while never actually dishonest, can be a bit of a sly fox when necessary. The quickest of all Dogs, the Gemini breed gets impatient when the going gets slow and resorts to the odd trick to speed things along. Nevertheless, these types are truthful and honest in their own way and have a knack of falling on their feet... whatever happens.

Cancer Dog

The Cancer Dog was born to be in a settled relationship. These types are never totally happy until they've found their true love and built a cozy home to snuggle up in together. Cancer Dog is not overly concerned with a career. As long as these types earn enough to pay the mortgage and buy life's essentials, they are happy. The right companionship is what they crave. With the perfect partner by their side, they are truly content.

Leo Dog

If Leo Dogs really did have four legs, chances are they would be police dogs. These types are sticklers for law and order. They will not tolerate injustice and will seek out wrongdoers and plague them until they change their ways. Woe betide any workmate who is pilfering pens, making free with office coffee or fiddling expenses. The Leo Dog will force them to own up and make amends. Should you be a victim of injustice, however, Leo Dog will zoom to your aid.

Virgo Dog

The Virgo Dog tends to be a great worrier. A born perfectionist, Virgo Dog agonizes over every detail and loses sleep if he suspects he has performed any task badly. These types are very clever and can achieve great things, but too often they fail to enjoy their success because they are too busy worrying they might have made a mistake. The crazy thing is, they very seldom do.

Libra Dog

The Libra Dog believes in 'live and let live'. A laid back, tolerant fellow, Libra Dog likes to lie in the sun and not interfere with anyone. Let sleeping dogs lie is definitely her motto. She will agree to almost anything for a quiet life. Yet it's unwise to push her too far. When there's no alternative, this particular hound can produce a very loud bark.

Scorpio Dog

The Scorpio Dog is as loyal and trustworthy as other canines, but more difficult to get to know. Beneath that amiable exterior is a very suspicious heart. These types don't quite understand why they are so wary of others, but it takes them a long time to learn to trust. Perhaps they are afraid of getting hurt. The idea of marriage fills them with terror, and it takes a very patient partner to get them to the altar. Once married, however, they will be faithful and true.

Sagittarius Dog

The Sagittarius Dog is inexhaustible. These cheerful types are always raring to go and quite happy to join in with any adventure. They love to be part of the gang and are perfectly willing to follow someone else's lead. They don't mind if their ideas are not always accepted; they just like being involved. These types work splendidly in teams and can achieve great things in a group.

Capricorn Dog

The Capricorn Dog is a very caring type. These subjects are happy so long as their loved ones are happy, but they greatly fear that a friend or family member might fall ill. This concern, probably kept secret, gives them real anxiety and should a loved one show worrying symptoms, the Capricorn Dog will suffer sleepless nights until the problem is resolved. When they are not urging their families to keep warm and put on an extra vest, these types are likely to be out and about helping others less fortunate than themselves.

Aquarius Dog

The Aquarius Dog, when young, spends a great deal of time searching for a worthy cause to which they can become devoted. Since there are so many worthy causes from which to choose these types can suffer much heartache as they struggle to pick the right one. When – at last – a niche is found, however, the Aquarius Dog will settle down to a truly contented life of quiet satisfaction. These types need to serve and feel that they are improving life for others. This is their path to happiness.

Pisces Dog

Like the Aquarius breed, the Pisces Dog often has a number of false starts early in life although these are more likely to be of a romantic rather than philanthropic nature. The Pisces Dog wants to find a soulmate but is not averse to exploring a few cul-de-sacs on the way.

These types are not promiscuous, however, and when they do find Mr or Miss Right, they are blissfully happy to settle down.

Pig

Aries Pig

The Aries Pig always seems to wear a smile on its face and no wonder. Everything seems to go right for these cheerful types, and they scarcely seem to have to lift a finger to make things fall perfectly into place. In fact, of course, their good luck is the result of sheer hard work, but the Aries Pig has a knack of making work look like play so that nobody realizes the effort Pig is putting in.

Taurus Pig

Most Pigs are happy, but the Taurus Pigs really seem quite blissful most of the time. One of their favorite occupations is eating, and they delight in dreaming up sumptuous menus and then creating them for the enjoyment of themselves and their friends. For this reason, Taurus Pigs have a tendency to put on weight. Despite the time they devote to their hobby, however, Taurus Pigs usually do well in their career. Many gifted designers are born under this sign.

Gemini Pig

The Gemini Pig has a brilliant business brain gift-wrapped in a charming, happy go lucky personality. These types usually zoom straight to the top of their chosen tree, but they manage to do so smoothly and easily without ruffling too many feathers on the way. They are popular with their workmates, and later their employees, and nobody can figure out how quite such a nice, down to earth type has ended up in such a position of authority.

Cancer Pig

The Cancer Pig likes to give the impression of being a very hard working type. She is hard working, of course, but perhaps not quite as excessively as she likes others to believe. Secretly, the Cancer Pig makes sure there's plenty of time to spare for fun and indulgence. To the outside world, however, Pig pretends to be constantly slaving away and likes to get regular appreciation for these efforts.

Leo Pig

The Leo Pig is delightful company. Friendly, amusing and very warm and approachable. These types do however have a tremendously lazy streak. Left to themselves, they would not rise till noon, and they prefer someone else to do all the cleaning and cooking. The Leo Pig has to be nagged to make an effort, but when these types do so, they can achieve impressive results.

Virgo Pig

The Virgo Pig, in contrast, is a highly conscientious creature. These types can't abide laziness, and while they are normally kindly, helpful souls who gladly assist others, they will not lift a finger to aid someone who has brought his problems on himself through slovenliness. The Virgo Pig is a clean, contented type who usually achieves a happy life.

Libra Pig

The creative Libra Pig is always dreaming up new ways to improve their home. These types love to be surrounded by beautiful and comfortable things but seldom get round to completing their ideas because they are having such a good time in other ways. This is probably just as well because the minute they decide on one color scheme, they suddenly see something that might work better. A permanent work in progress is probably the best option.

Scorpio Pig

The Scorpio Pig usually goes far. The amiable Pig boosted by powerful, almost psychic Scorpio can seem turbo-charged at times. These types keep their own counsel more than their chatty cousins, and this often stands them in good stead in business. They can be a little too cautious at times, but they rarely make mistakes.

Sagittarius Pig

Eat, drink and be merry is the motto of the Sagittarius Pig. These types have the intelligence to go far in their careers but, in truth, they would rather party. They love to dress up, get together with a bunch of friends and laugh and dance until dawn. Sagittarius Pig hates to be alone for long, so is always off in search of company.

Capricorn Pig

Pigs are normally broad-minded types, but the Capricorn Pig is a little more staid than his cousins. Nevertheless, being able to narrow their vision gives these types the ability to channel their concentration totally onto the subject in hand, a gift which is vital to success in many professions. For this reason, Capricorn Pigs often make a name for themselves in their chosen career.

Aquarius Pig

Honest, straightforward and popular Aquarius Pigs have more friends than they can count. Always good-humored and cheerful these types gravitate to those in need and do whatever they can to help. The Aquarius Pig gives copiously to charity and frequently wishes to do more. These types tend to have their heads in the clouds most of the time and for this reason, tend not to give their careers or finances the attention they should. But since worldly success means little to the Aquarius Pig, this hardly matters.

Pisces Pig

The Pisces Pig is a particularly sweet-natured creature. These types are real dreamers. They float around in a world of their own, and people tend to make allowances for them. Yet, from time to time, the Pisces Pig drifts in from his other planet to startle everyone with a stunningly brilliant idea. There is more to the Pisces Pig than meets the eye.

Rat

Aries Rat

Fiery Aries adds more than usual urgency to the sociable Rat. While these types enjoy company, they also tend to be impatient and can get quite bad-tempered and aggressive with anyone who seems to waste their time. Aries Rats do not suffer fools and will stomp off on their own if someone annoys them. In fact, this is the best thing all round. Aries Rats hate to admit it, but they benefit from a little solitude which enables them to calm down and recharge their batteries. Happily, as quickly as these types flare up, they just as quickly cool off again.

Taurus Rat

When Taurus, renowned for a love of luxury and the finer things in life, is born in a comfort-loving Rat year, a true gourmet and bon viveur has entered the world. The Taurus effect enhances the sensuous parts of the Rat personality and lifts them to new heights. Good food is absolutely essential to these types. They don't eat to live; they really do live to eat. Many excellent chefs are born under this sign, and even those folks who don't make catering their career are likely to be outstanding home cooks. Dinner parties thrown by Taurus Rats are memorable affairs. The only drawback with these types is that they can become a little pernickety and overly fussy about details. They also have to watch their weight.

Gemini Rat

While Taurus accentuates the Rat's love of good living, Gemini heightens the Rat's already well-developed social skills. That crowd chuckling and laughing around the witty type in the corner are bound to be listening to a Gemini Rat. Amusing, quick-thinking, and never lost for words, the only things likely to drive Gemini Rats away are bores and undue seriousness. Gemini Rats prefer light, entertaining conversation and head for the hills when things get too heavy. Delightful as they always are however, it is difficult to capture the attention of a Gemini Rat for long. These types love to circulate. They make an entrance and then move on to pastures new. Pinning them down never works. They simply lose interest and with it that famous sparkle.

Cancer Rat

Cancer makes the Rat a little more sensitive and easily hurt than usual. These types are emotional and loving but sometimes come across as martyrs. They work hard but tend to feel, often without good cause, their efforts are not as well appreciated as they should be. Cancer Rats frequently suspect they are being taken for granted at home and at work, but their love of company prevents them from making too big a fuss. Rats are naturally gifted business people, and the Cancer Rat has a particularly good head for financial affairs. These types enjoy working with others, and they are especially well suited to partnerships. However, don't expect the sensitive, feeling Cancer Rat to be a pushover. These types can be surprisingly demanding at work and will not tolerate any laziness on the part of employees.

Leo Rat

Leo Rats usually get to the top. Few people can resist them. The combination of Rat sociability, business acumen and ambition, coupled with extrovert Leo's rather, shall we say, 'pushy', qualities and flair for leadership can't help but power these types to the top of whatever tree they happen to choose to climb. Along the way, however, they may irritate those few less gifted souls who fail to fall under their spell. Such doubters may complain that Leo Rat hogs the limelight and tends to become overbearing at times but since hardly anyone else seems to notice, why should Leo Rat care?

Virgo Rat

As we have already seen, the delightful Rat does have a stingy streak in his make-up, and when the astrological sign of Virgo is added to the mix, this characteristic tends to widen. At best, Virgo Rats are terrific savers and do wonders with their investments. The Rat tendency to squander money on unwise bargains is almost entirely absent in these types, and they often end up seriously rich. At worst, however, in negative types, Virgo Rats can be real Scrooges, grating the last sliver of soap to save on washing powder, sitting in the dark to conserve electricity and attempting their own shoe repairs with stick-on soles, even when they have plenty of money in the bank. Virgo Rats are brilliant at detail; but in negative types, they put this gift to poor use spending far too long on money-saving schemes when they would do much better to look for ways of expanding their income.

Libra Rat

The Libra Rat adores company even more than most. In fact, these types are seldom alone. They have dozens of friends, their phones never stop ringing, and most evenings the Libra Rat is entertaining. Libra Rat enjoys civilized gatherings rather than wild parties and friends will be treated to beautiful music, exquisite food and a supremely comfortable home. These types really can charm the birds off the trees, not with the brilliant repartee of the Gemini Rat but with a warmth and low key humor all their own. These types do tend to be a touch lazier than the usual Rat and their weakness for bargains, particularly in the areas of art and fashion, is more pronounced, but their charm is so strong that partners forgive them for overspending.

Scorpio Rat

It's often said that Rats would make good journalists or detectives because beneath that expansive surface is a highly observant brain. Well the best of them all would be the Rat born under Scorpio. A veritable Sherlock Holmes of a Rat if you wish to be flattering, or a real nosey parker if you don't. These types are endlessly curious. They want to know everything that's going on, who is doing what with whom where and for how long. They may not have any particular use for the information they gather, but they just can't help gathering it all the same. Scorpio Rats often have psychic powers though they may not be aware of this and these powers aid them in their 'research'. Unlike other Rats, those born under Scorpio prefer their own company and like to work alone. When they manage to combine their curiosity and talent for digging out information, there is almost no limit to what they can achieve with their career

Sagittarius Rat

Traditionally Rats have many friends, but the Sagittarius Rat has the not so welcome distinction of collecting a few enemies along the way as well. The Sagittarius Rat finds this quite extraordinary as he never intends to upset anyone. It's just that these types can be forthright to the point of rudeness and an affable nature can only compensate so far. These types are amicable and warm, but when they speak their minds, some people never forgive them. Despite this tendency, Sagittarius Rats have a knack for accumulating money and plough it back into their business to good effect. They manage to be generous, and a bit mean at the same time, which baffles their friends, but those that have not been offended by Sagittarius Rat's tactless tongue tend to stay loyal forever.

Capricorn Rat

Rats are naturally high achievers, but perhaps the highest achiever of them all is likely to be born under the sign of Capricorn. These types are not loud and brilliant like Leo Rats. They tend to be quietly ambitious. They keep in the background, watching what needs to be done, astutely judging who counts and who does not, and then when they are absolutely sure they are on solid ground, they move in. After such preparation, they are unlikely to make a mistake, but if they do they blame themselves, they are bitterly angry, and they resolve never to repeat their stupidity. Reckless these types are not, but their methods produce good results, and they make steady progress towards their goals.

Aquarius Rat

All Rats are blessed with good brains, but few of them think of themselves as intellectuals. The exceptions are the Rats born under the sign of Aquarius. While being friendly and sociable, the Aquarian Rat also needs time alone to think things through and to study the latest subject that has aroused his interest. Perhaps not so adept at business as most Rats, those born under the sign of Aquarius make up for any deficiency in this department by teeming with good ideas. They are intuitive, very hard working and love to be involved in 'people' projects.

Pisces Rat

Pisces Rats tend to be quieter than their more flamboyant brothers and sisters. They are not drawn to the limelight, and they are not so interested in business as other Rats. In fact, working for other people has little appeal for them, although this is what they often end up doing through want of thinking up a better idea. Should a more enterprising Pisces Rat decide to put his mind to business, however, he will often end up self-employed which suits him extremely well. Having taken the plunge, many a self-employed Pisces Rat surprises himself by doing very well indeed. These types can be amazingly shrewd and intuitive, and once these powers are harnessed to the right career, they progress in leaps and bounds. Pisces Rats tend to do well in spite of themselves.

CHAPTER 17: CREATE A WONDERFUL YEAR

By now, you should have got a pretty good idea of the main influences on your life and personality, according to Chinese astrology. But how is 2021 going to shape up for you? Well, that largely depends on how cleverly you play your hand.

The Year of the Ox is traditionally a calmer, more measured year than the Rat year it follows. This is a time where hard work and discipline are rewarded and family values become more important.

Some signs will find these conditions more comfortable than others. Zodiac creatures that prefer to think things over carefully, before making a move, will thrive; energetic, always-in-a-hurry types could find themselves irritated. Yet, as long as you're prepared – and you know what you might be up against – you can develop plans to ride those waves like a world-class surfer.

Sit back and rely on good fortune alone, because it's a terrific year for your sign, and you could snatch failure from the jaws of success. Navigate any stormy seas with skill and foresight, if it's not such a sunny year for your sign, and you'll sail on to fulfil your dreams. This is always true in any year, but doubly so when careful Ox is in charge. Above all, the Ox encourages sincere effort and patient persistence. So no matter what zodiac sign you were born under, 'Ox year energy' will help you if you help yourself.

The future is not set in stone.

Chinese astrology is used very much like a weather forecast, so that you can check out the likely conditions you'll encounter on your journey and plan your route and equipment accordingly. Some signs might need a parasol and sandals; while others, stout walking boots and rain-gear. Yet, properly prepared, both will end up in a good place at the end of the trip.

Finally, it's said that if you feel another sign has a much better outlook than you this year, you can carry a small symbol of that animal with you (in the form of a piece of jewelry, perhaps, or a tiny charm in your pocket or bag) and their good luck will rub off on you. Does it work? For some, maybe, but there's certainly no harm in trying.

Other Top-Rated Books

Linda Dearsley – *the author of this book* – was Doris Stokes' ghost.

Well, more accurately, she was the ghost-writer for Doris Stokes and worked with her for 10 years to produce 7 books, detailing the great lady's life.

In Voices Everywhere, Linda shines a light on her time working with Doris, right from the very early days when Doris was doing private readings in her Fulham flat, to filling the London Palladium and Barbican night after night, to subsequent fame outside the UK. Throughout all this, Doris Stokes never became anyone other than who she was: a kind, generous, and down-to-earth woman with an extraordinary gift, and a fondness for a nice cup of tea. January 6th, 2020, would have been Doris' 100th birthday.

Following Doris' death, Linda chronicles how cynics tried to torpedo the Stokes legacy with accusations of cheating and dishonesty, but how those closest to Doris never believed she was anything other than genuine.

In turn, as the months and years rolled by, more and more intriguing people crossed Linda's path, each with their own unexplainable power, and Doris never seemed far away. From the palmist who saw pictures in people's hands, to the couple whose marriage was predicted by Doris, and the woman who believes she captures departed spirits on camera – the mysterious world of the paranormal, and Doris Stokes' place within it, continues to unfold.

Karina Collins is an acclaimed Tarot reader who has helped people, from all walks of life, to better understand their lives' journeys.

Now, she is on a mission to help you take control of your life – through the power of Tarot – to better explore and understand your purpose and destiny.

Do you have questions about now and your future? Perhaps about making more money, or whether love is on the horizon, or whether you will become happier? Do you want to steer your life in a direction that brings success, pleasure, and fulfilment? Well, Tarot is a means to help you do exactly that! Used for centuries, it provides a powerful tool for unlocking knowledge, divining the future, and delivering shortcuts to the lives we desire.

In this full-colour book, Karina provides explanations and insights into the full 78-card Tarot deck, how to phrase questions most effectively, real-world sample readings, why seemingly scary cards represent opportunities for growth and triumph, and more.

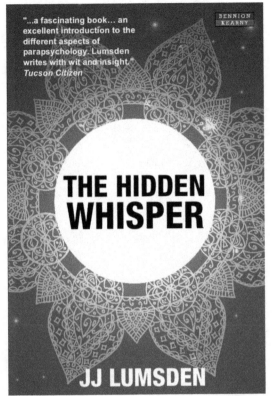

A paranormal puzzle smoulders in the desert heat of southern Arizona. At the home of Jack and Chloe Monroe, a written message "Leave Now" appears then disappears, a candle in an empty room mysteriously lights itself, and – most enigmatically – an unidentifiable ethereal whisper begins to permeate the house. What was once simply strange now feels sinister. What once seemed a curiosity now seems terrifying.

Dr. Luke Jackson, a British Parapsychologist visiting family nearby, is asked to investigate and quickly finds himself drawn deeper into the series of unexplained events. Time is against him. He has just one week to understand and resolve the poltergeist case before he must depart Arizona.

The Hidden Whisper is the acclaimed paranormal thriller, written by real-life parapsychologist Dr. JJ Lumsden, which offers a rare opportunity to enter the intriguing world of parapsychology through the eyes of Luke Jackson. The fictional narrative is combined with extensive endnotes and references that cover Extra Sensory Perception, Psychokinesis, Haunts, Poltergeists, Out of Body Experiences, and more. If you thought parapsychology was like Ghostbusters – think again...

"This book works on many levels, an excellent introduction to the concepts current in the field of parapsychology... at best you may learn something new, and at worst you'll have read a witty and well-written paranormal detective story" Parascience.

www.BennionKearny.com/paranormal

CPSIA information can be obtained
at www.ICGtesting.com
Printed in the USA
LVHW080753070321
680783LV00004B/24